Sherman IC
Firefly

Wojciech J. Gawrych

Model Centrum PROGRES   www.modelbooks.republika.pl

SHERMAN IC FIREFLY

Wojciech J. Gawrych

Published by Model Centrum Progres, Poland
Warsaw, July 2009

Copyright © 2009 by Model Centrum Progres
www.modelbooks.republika.pl
medelbooks@op.pl

Text © 2009 Wojciech J. Gawrych
Scale plans © 2009 Krzysztof M. Żurek
Current color photos © 2009 William Marshall
Front cover art © 2009 Arkadiusz Wróbel
Historical photo credits: Barry Beldam Collection; Daniele Guglielmi Collection; Steve Guthrie Collection; Zbigniew Lalak Collection; William Marshall Collection; Jeffrey Plowman Collection; Steven J. Zaloga Collection; DND Army; SANDF Archives; Polish Institute and Sikorski Museum, London via Andrzej A. Kamiński [PISM]; Imperial War Museum; Public Archives of Canada; Tank Museum

English proof-reading by Roger Lucy and Paul Roberts

Acknowledgments
The Author and Editor wishes to express his thanks to Krzysztof Barbarski, President of the Polish Institute and Sikorski Museum, London, U.K.; Barry Beldam, Kingston, Canada; Michael Franz, Korschenbroich, Germany; Daniele Guglielmi, Calenzano, Italy; Steve Guthrie, Peterborough, Canada; Richard Henry, SA National Museum of Military History, Johannesburg, South Africa; Andrzej A. Kamiński, Cracow, Poland; Zbigniew Lalak, Warsaw, Poland; Kurt Laughlin, Beaver Falls, PA, USA; William Marshall, Pretoria, South Africa; Jeffrey Plowman, Christchurch, New Zealand

All rights reserved by Model Centrum Progres, Warsaw, Poland. No part of this book may be reproduced or transmitted in any form or by any means, electronic or mechanical, including photocopying, recording or by any information storage retrieval system, without permission in writing from the Publisher.

ISBN 978-83-60672-10-5

Edited by Wojciech J. Gawrych
Cover layout, design and layout by
PROGRES Publishing House, Warsaw
DTP and prepress by AIRES-GRAF, Warsaw
Printed and bound in European Union by REGIS Ltd.,
Napoleona 4, 05-230 Kobyłka, Poland

Sherman Hybrid IC Firefly

National Museum of Military History – Johannesburg, South Africa

1 The Sherman Hybrid IC Firefly belonging to the collection of the South African National Museum of Military History in Saxonwold, Johannesburg, South Africa.

This vehicle came off the production line at the American Locomotive Company, Schenectady, NY in October 1943 as Tank, Medium, M4, with hull or serial number 40319 and was allocated the U.S. Army registration number USA 3072916. This M4, with a 75 mm gun, was later modified by the Detroit Tank Arsenal with a combination cast nose section fitted onto a welded hull and so became in U.S. nomenclature an M4 Composite Hull. Only a very few vehicles were converted after they had been completed as standard M4s, so this is an exceptionally rare Sherman.

After completion as a composite hull Sherman, this tank was supplied to the British as part of British contract S/M 1046 for 2,000 Sherman tanks. It was allocated British W.D. number T-263727. The Chilwell Schedule lists these 2,000 tanks as having been allocated the British Registration Numbers T-261894 to T-263893 so this Museum's Sherman falls within the correct sequence of numbers. This tank was selected to become a 17-pdr armed Sherman Firefly and was converted late in 1944 (most likely in November/December), probably at the Royal Ordnance Factory at Radcliffe. During conversion the tank was fitted with the British 17-pdr Mk. VII gun manufactured by Royal Ordnance Factory at Leeds. With the new potent gun, the British name for the type changed to Sherman Hybrid IC Firefly.

It is believed that this tank served with the 6th South African Armored Division in Italy. The first armored unit of 11th Armored Brigade (6 Div) to receive their Fireflies was the Special Service Battalion in November 1944. The Pretoria Regiment and Prince Alfred Guard received their Fireflies later, with the last ones received in January 1945. They were used in Italy until 14 May 1945 when the whole division took part in a Victory Parade at the Monza Raceway (Autodromo di Monza). After this parade, most 6th Armored Division vehicles, apart from the troop carrying trucks, were handed in to the reception depot at the Monza Raceway and stored there. Later the armored and soft skinned vehicles were transported by rail to the newly established 6th South African Armored Division Vehicle Park at Genoa. At the vehicle park, vehicles were serviced and repaired.

The South African authorities had to work through British channels and agreement was reached as to the type and quantity of equipment required by the post war Union Defense Forces (UDF). From the vehicles that were shipped to South Africa in 1946/47, it appears that a selection of the best condition vehicles was made from all the available "British" equipment. The Sherman Firefly bearing the British W.D. number T-263727 was allocated the UDF Registration Number U 74937. It appears that this number was painted on the tank at the 6th South African Armored Division Vehicle Park, Genoa, while waiting to be shipped to South Africa.

In May 1948, U 74937, the Museum's Sherman Firefly, appeared as one of eight Fireflies on issue to 1 Special Service Battalion at Potchefstroom. After 1962 the Firefly was repainted in a PFU Olive Drab Semi-Gloss. During this painting, the SADF personnel applied the Republic of South Africa registration prefix R to the tank. The R prefix replaced the U prefix, but the registration number was to remain unchanged. Someone however mixed up the numbers and the incorrect registration number R 74994 was applied. In a Strength Return of AFVs at 81 Technical Stores Depot, Lylletton, Pretoria dated 31 March 1970, the Museum's Sherman Firefly was still one of fourteen listed on charge to this unit.

In about 1976 the Firefly was donated by the South African Defense Force to the Military Museum, Fort Klapperkop. When Fort Klapperkop was closed in mid-1992, this Sherman Firefly was donated to the South African National Museum of Military History where it arrived on 22 June 1993.

In November/December 2006 the Museum's Firefly was cleaned, the interior painted in white enamel and the exterior in the British S.C.C. No. 15 Olive Drab to represent the color used in Italy in November 1944 – May 1945. When the paint was sanded down, layer by layer, a yellow outlined diamond, the tactical sign for HQ Squadron was discovered on the turret sides. Inside the diamond shape was a blue color which closely matches the BSI 381C of 1964 color number 107 "Strong Blue". Since it resembled marking systems used by tanks of the South African Pretoria Regiment during the Italian campaign in 1944-45, the Museum decided to paint their Sherman Firefly exhibit in the colors of the Pretoria Regiment – a white 52 on a red square background of size 8 in. x 8 in. This was painted on the right side final drive bulge and the 6th South African Armored Division flash on the left final drive bulge. The British W.D. Number T-263737 was applied in white paint to the rear, on either side.

Armor PhotoGallery

2 The front lower hull. The one-piece differential and final drive housing is of the late production type. This type of the housing had a more pointed beak than the earlier design. This change was done to provide more room for the double brake system's components used on late tanks.

3 Foundry marks visible on the differential and final drive housing. The letter "G" enclosed within an octagon denotes the American Steel Foundries, Granite City (Illinois) Works. The U.S. Ordnance Department part number, E8543, indicates that this is the late production differential and final drive housing fitted with the double anchor brake system while B1004 is the casting pattern number.

4 The middle part of the differential and final drive housing. Note the remains of the spare track brackets that held three links.

5 The right side twin towing lugs. The step, normally welded between the outer lug and the final drive bulge, is missing from this vehicle.

Armor PhotoGallery

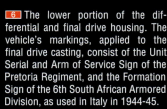

6 The lower portion of the differential and final drive housing. The vehicle's markings, applied to the final drive casting, consist of the Unit Serial and Arm of Service Sign of the Pretoria Regiment, and the Formation Sign of the 6th South African Armored Division, as used in Italy in 1944-45.

7 Overhead view of the glacis and the differential and final drive housing.
8 Close-up view showing the profile of the bolt protecting lip at the top of the differential and final drive housing. This feature was introduced early in the production of the single-piece differential and final drive housing.
9 Front view of the differential and final drive housing. Note the sharp front edge of the casting.
10 The left side twin lugs for towing incorporating the step for the crew. The front of the tow cable was normally shackled to the left front towing device. This eliminated the front hold down bracket installed atop of the front casting that appeared in earlier tanks.

ARMOR PHOTOGALLERY

11 The right front view of the glacis. In this type of the M4 Sherman, known as a Composite Hull M4 or Sherman Hybrid, only the front of the hull was cast, with the rest of the hull assembled from welded flat plates. The front casting was revised during production to incorporate the larger hatches common to late war tanks, like this one. The glacis was 51 mm (2 in.) thick in front with a nominal slope of 51 degrees from vertical.

12 The right front glacis. The armored plug was welded over the bow machine gun hole. The pyramid-like shape of the plug is clearly visible on the photo. Note the weld beads where the ball mount cover fixture had previously been fitted to the glacis.

13 Close-up view of the right lifting eye, and the right headlight's brush guard. The headlights were easily removed to protect them during combat by unplugging the wires inside the tank and unscrewing the headlights from their mounts. Plugs were provided to seal up the holes when the headlights were removed.

14 The gun travel lock mount for the 75 mm gun. The 75 mm gun travel lock was deleted when the tank was converted into a 17-pdr Firefly.

Armor PhotoGallery

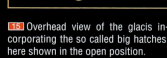

15 Overhead view of the glacis incorporating the so called big hatches, here shown in the open position.

16 17 Two views of the siren guard and left headlight brush guard. The siren was relocated to be in front of the driver in later production tanks.

18 Close-up view of the left lifting eye. Made of cast steel, it has the flared legs typical for 47 degrees hull tanks.

19 The left front fender.

20 The upper glacis. The driver and co-drivers each had a rotating M6 periscope mounted in the hatch and a fixed M6 periscope mounted in the hull roof in front of the hatch.

21 The armored cover for the SCR 506 radio antenna socket. These radios were normally installed only in command tanks.

22 The co-driver's hatch cover. The rotating M6 periscope has the protective guard which was added to later-production Shermans.

23 The U-shaped slot to allow airflow into the ventilator mounted below the front hull roof between the drivers. The thin cover for the fixed M6 periscope is missing.

24 Close-up view of the co-driver's periscope.

25 26 Two overhead views of the co-driver's periscope. Note the hinge details.

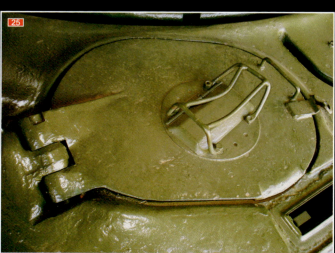

Armor PhotoGallery

[27] Overhead view of the glacis incorporating the big hatches, here shown in closed position.

[28] The foundry marks located on the cast hull roof just outboard of the driver's hatch. The letter "C" enclosed within an octagon denotes the American Steel Foundries Cast Armor Plant, East Chicago, Indiana, the U.S. Ordnance Department part number is E6289, and the pattern number is A238. "LO" is believed to indicate a particular type of heat treatment.

[29] Overhead view of the driver's hatch. Note the weather hood clips on either side of the driver's periscope. The metal cover was mounted over the U-shaped slot in late production tanks.

[30] Inner side of the driver's hatch showing the periscope mount. The U.S. Ordnance Department part number for the driver's hatch was D82050A, while the co-driver's hatch, a mirror-image design, had part number D82050B.

[31] The front upper glacis. Note the upper catch for the gun travel lock.

Armor PhotoGallery

[32] The left front hull sponson showing the bulkhead, the tool storage box and the main instrument panel. The roof top ventilator is visible in the foreground (above the instrument panel).

[33] The cooker storage rack located in the left sponson behind the driver's seat.
[34] The tool storage box located in the left sponson to the left of the driver's seat.
[35] Upper portion of the steering levers and the hand grips.
[36] Overhead view of the driver's seat less its cushion and seat back. The top of the gearshift lever can be seen on the right side of the driver's seat with a push button for shifting into reverse on top of the handle knob.

[37] Lower portion of the steering levers and the floor of the drivers' compartment. The main accelerator pedal is visible down to the left of the transmission housing, and the clutch pedal is to the left of steering levers. Steering was via a controlled differential using conventional steering levers. Rods from the driver's steering levers connected to the steering brake shaft levers, the left lever connected directly to the shaft lever on the driver's side of the tank. The right steering lever connected to the steering brake cross shaft which transferred the rotating movement to the assistant driver's side of the case, where it was connected to the right steering brake control rod. The companion flange at the back of the transmission connected to the driveshaft from the engine.

Armor PhotoGallery

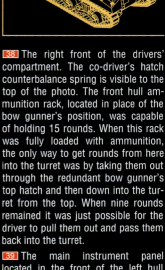

38 The right front of the drivers' compartment. The co-driver's hatch counterbalance spring is visible to the top of the photo. The front hull ammunition rack, located in place of the bow gunner's position, was capable of holding 15 rounds. When this rack was fully loaded with ammunition, the only way to get rounds from here into the turret was by taking them out through the redundant bow gunner's top hatch and then down into the turret from the top. When nine rounds remained it was just possible for the driver to pull them out and pass them back into the turret.

39 The main instrument panel located in the front of the left hull sponson. The instrument panel for each Sherman type was different, depending on the engine used. This one was repainted in white, but panels were typically dark green or black, and most of the dials had black faces with white printing.

40 Close-up view of the roof top ventilator, seen from the driver's side.

41 A mechanism located on the rear top surface of the transmission housing. The driver's seat appears behind it. The oblique racks for .50 cal. ammunition are located behind the driver's seat

42 The bow machine gun mount, plugged from outside with a block of armor plate. Below is visible the right end of the steering-brake cross-shaft located in top of the transmission/steering unit, and the front of the front hull ammunition rack. To the left, mounted above the transmission, is the large shelf for storing the driver's foul weather hood. This could be attached to the hatch above the driver.

Armor PhotoGallery

43 The left front view of Johannesburg's vehicle showing the left hull sponson.

44 The rear of the left hull sponson showing the tank's original W.D. Number, T-263727.

45 The left hull appliqué armor plate. This 25.4 mm (1 in.) thick plate was trimmed to clear the glacis weld. The hull appliqué armor plates were factory installed on the Chrysler-rebuilt Composite hull tanks like this one.

46 The auxiliary generator fuel filler cap (left) and the fuel filler cap located behind the turret ring. The turret splash rail is bent inboard to form the rear protection for the auxiliary generator fuel filler port. Later in the production, the rear section was made a separate piece welded to the side rail.

47 The rear of the turret ring splash rail; note the two drain holes and the bracket for the tow cable.

48 Overhead view of the auxiliary generator fuel filler cap (right) and the outboard fuel filler cap (middle).

49 The rear left sponson showing the fire extinguisher mount pad, the lifting eye, the tail light and its brush guard, and the tow cable's bracket. Two Pyrene fire extinguishers were common external stowage on all British & Commonwealth Shermans. These were replaced by methyl bromide extinguishers later in the war. The grouser box cover is missing allowing a view inside it.

Armor PhotoGallery

50 51 Two views of the fitted stowage box typical for South African Hybrid IC Fireflies operating in Italy from late 1944 until the war's end.
52 Side view of the rear left sponson and its fittings.
53 The auxiliary generator fuel filler cap (below) and the two fuel filler caps (above) located behind the turret ring. In later production tanks of this type, the inboard fuel filler caps were deleted. This simplified the design and may have reduced engine fires slightly.
54 Overhead view of the rear left sponson and its fittings.

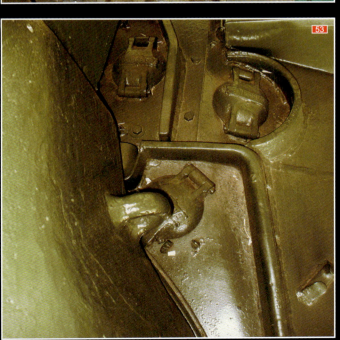

Armor PhotoGallery

55 A right front view of the museum vehicle showing the right hull sponson.

56 The aft end of the right sponson showing the tank's W.D. Number.
57 View of the right sponson top plate showing the arrangement of the tool brackets. The tool brackets for the track bar, mattock handle, shovel, mattock and ax were welded on top of the right sponson in all welded hull Sherman models.

58 Overhead view of the rear left sponson and its fittings.
59 The appliqué armor plate welded to the rear of the right sponson. This trapezoidal plate measures 813 x 537 x 429 mm (32 x 21.125 x 16.875 in.).

60 Side view of the rear left sponson and its fittings.
61 Close-up view of the brush guard and the right taillight.

ARMOR PHOTOGALLERY

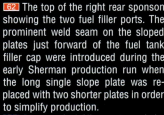

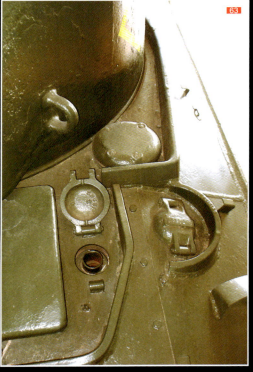

62 The top of the right rear sponson showing the two fuel filler ports. The prominent weld seam on the sloped plates just forward of the fuel tank filler cap were introduced during the early Sherman production run when the long single slope plate was replaced with two shorter plates in order to simplify production.

63 The two fuel filler ports and the rear rooftop ventilator cover; note the asymmetrical arrangement of the screw heads.

64 The tool stowage brackets fitted to the right middle sponson top plate.

65 The right front top sponson plate and the turret ring splash guard; note the arrangement of the weld beads and the two drain holes in the rear splash guard.

66 Close-up view of the outboard fuel filler cap fitted with the identification placard for gasoline.

67 The appliqué armor plate which the Detroit Tank Arsenal (Chrysler) welded to the front of the right sponson when the tank was converted to the composite hull configuration by replacing the original welded hull front plates with a cast nose section welded to the rear hull. The appliqué plate was cut diagonally to allow it to lie against the front hull casting. Note the rounded upper right corner of the right-hand appliqué plate.

Armor PhotoGallery

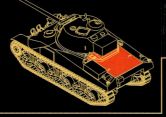

68 The left side view of the engine deck. This configuration is typical to all radial-engined Shermans, whether armed with the 75 mm, 76 mm or 17-pdr guns. The rearmost engine deck plate is welded to the upper sponson and the rear hull plates. The two forward engine deck plates could be removed for routine service. The middle plate (hinged) was removed from the Johannesburg vehicle providing an excellent view into the engine compartment.

69 Close-up view of the box-like armored cover which protects the fire extinguisher pull handles. Note the mounting screw for the front deck plate visible in the foreground.

70 Rear view of the front deck plate with the armored cover for the inlet air grill.

Armor PhotoGallery

73 The right side view of the engine deck. The forward engine deck plate includes a screened rectangular hole which is the air inlet. The screen over the inlet is further protected by a heavy armored cover that is hinged at the rear to allow the screen to be cleaned. The middle engine plate is missing from the Johannesburg vehicle. It was hinged onto the front plate and had two lifting handles. It was fastened with three bolts along the rear edge.

74 The armored cover and the splash rail providing protection for the two inner fuel filler ports and the air inlet grill.

75 The left inner fuel filler (open). The filler could also be used to check the fuel level manually by inserting a dipstick into the filler tube.

76 Right side view of the armored cover and its splash guard; note details of the air inlet screen mesh. The engine cooling fan is located immediately below the inlet screen.

71 72 Two views of the rearmost deck plate. Note the mounting brackets for the 17-pdr gun travel lock (actually missing from this vehicle). The gun travel lock was located at the back since the 17-pdr gun overhang was 1.4 m (55 in.), and the tank normally traveled with the turret reversed. The travel lock was offset to the left to prevent the driver's hatch from being blocked by the radio box in the turret rear.

Armor PhotoGallery

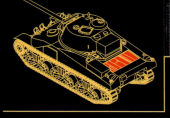

77 Overhead view of the engine compartment looking through the middle engine plate hatch. This tank was powered by a Continental R975 C1, 9-cylinder, 4-cycle, radial, air-cooled, petrol engine developing 400 hp (298 kW). The engine number is 304998 and the corresponding date of manufacture is 18 April 1945. Since it would have been impossible for the logistics system to have supplied this engine and the technical services to have fitted this engine before hostilities ended, it seems likely that this Firefly was re-engined sometime after the end of the war. The two pipes in the center of the photo are the two mufflers sitting on the muffler support located between them. The two pipes located each near the sides of the compartment are the right upper air intake tube and the left upper air intake tube respectively.

Armor PhotoGallery

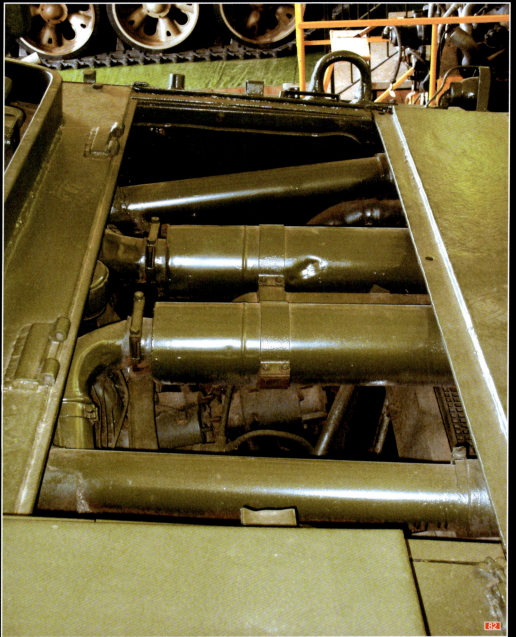

78 79 Two views into the rear of the engine compartment. The exhaust screen located under the rear hull overhang is visible deeper in both photos. Note the rear of each air intake filter is connected to the two air intake tubes: upper and lower.

80 81 Two views into the right area of the engine compartment. The right fuel tank is located behind the engine compartment's wall.

82 Left side view of the engine compartment, with the two mufflers appearing in the center of the photo. The earliest M3/M4/M4A1 tanks were powered with the Continental R975 EC2 which was originally designed as a Wright Whirlwind aero engine and used the 91 octane gasoline. By modifying the magnetos and lowering compression ratio from 6.3:1 to 5.7:1, the new engine, the R975 C1, was able to use 80 octane gasoline while developing the same power. The R975 C1 was produced in quantity by Continental Motors Corporation in Michigan.

83 A view into the front of the engine compartment. The breather is located atop the engine. The exhaust manifold for cylinders 1, 2, 3 and 4 is in the right and the exhaust manifold for cylinders 5, 6, 7, 8 and 9 is in the left.

84 Front of the engine compartment. The cooling air was blown back toward the cylinders (air cooled) and exhausted through the exhaust screen located under the rear hull overhang. The vanes of the engine cooling fan appear in the background of the photo.

Armor PhotoGallery

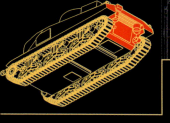

85 The rear upper hull plate sloped at 10 degrees to the vertical. Note the British pattern first aid box located to the left side of the plate.

86 The left rear end of the hull showing the cylindrical air filter.

87 Close-up view of the British-pattern first aid box.

88 The adjustable eccentric shaft assembly of the left idler wheel mount, and the left twin tow lugs.

89 The mounting brackets for the British-style leaf spring towing hook that spanned the rear plate. This was the usual type of tow hitch seen on the majority of Shermans including Fireflies. A matching set of brackets is fitted on the opposite side of the engine door.

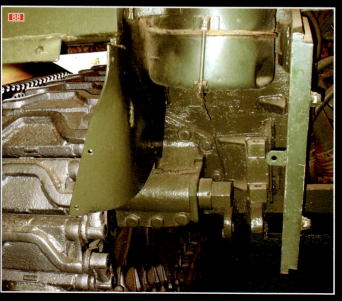

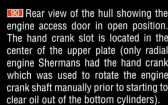

90 Rear view of the hull showing the engine access door in open position. The hand crank slot is located in the center of the upper plate (only radial engine Shermans had the hand crank which was used to rotate the engine crank shaft manually prior to starting to clear oil out of the bottom cylinders).

91 Underside view of the rear hull overhang showing the air outlet screen and how the exhaust pipes protrude aft of the screen.

92 Inner side of the right engine compartment door.

93 Rear view into the engine compartment. The two air intake ducts are seen arriving at the carburetor at the bottom of the engine. The ducts originate from the air cleaners and connect

to the carburetor assembly. Above the carburetor is the fuel pump, with fuel lines coming in from a number of different directions. The round component attached to the left side of the pump is the engine speed governor. The generator is mounted centrally with flanking magnetos, and the light-colored, uniquely shaped object is the engine mounting frame which extends to both sides where it attaches to the engine compartment walls.

94 The adjustable, eccentric shaft assembly of the right idler wheel mount.

95 Close-up view of the central tow bracket introduced on later production Shermans.

Armor PhotoGallery

96 The left side view of the Johannesburg Firefly showing the VVSS suspension components. The left side suspension consists of a mix of older spoked wheels as well as later stamped disc type road wheels. All three bogeys have horizontal return roller brackets with raised pillow blocks.

97 The left drive sprocket. This is the final production design which was simplified with a simple, circular hole for the inner diameter and the only finishing being performed on the outer profile. By 1945, this was the most common Sherman sprocket in use.

98 Close-up view of the front left bogey. This is the intermediate production VVSS bogey fitted with a horizontal return roller bracket fitted with the additional bearing pillow block to raise the roller. This bogey layout was very common on Sherman tanks in 1943-44 and remained in use to the end of the war.

99 100 Two oblique views of the intermediate production heavy duty VVSS bogey.

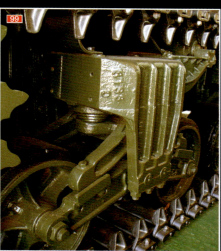

Armor PhotoGallery

101 The side face of the spring housing on the side of the bogey without the roller support bracket. Note the four prominent holes for bolting on a roller support bracket. Sherman bogey spring housings could be installed on either side of the tank; all that was necessary was to install the trailing arm on the proper side of the housing.

102 Close-up view of the solid spoke idler wheel introduced on later production vehicles.

103 Close-up view of the left middle bogey. This is again the intermediate production VVSS bogey.

104 Close-up view of the trailing arm and return roller mount with the bearing pillow block. This is a very early type of trailing arm that had cast-in reinforcing gussets.

105 Close-up view of the stamped spoked road wheel, the suspension lever and suspension arm.

106 Close-up view of the open spoke road wheel, the suspension lever and suspension arm.

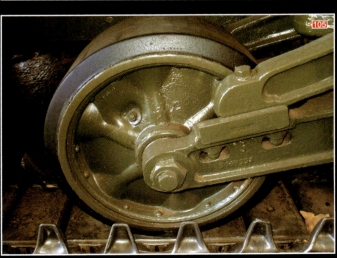
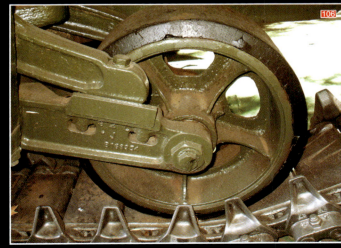

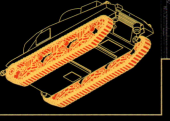

107 Close-up view of the left side solid spoke idler wheel. Note the relief valve and grease nipples, the casting marks on the dust caps, and the idler wheel mount bolted to the lower hull side.

108 Close-up view of the rear right bogey.
109 Close-up view of the right middle bogey.

110 111 Two oblique view of the intermediate production heavy duty VVSS bogey. The two 200 mm dia. volute springs were housed vertically inside the bracket casting and each acted on one of the two suspension levers. The levers pivoted inside the bogey bracket and supported the suspension arms. Contact between the arm and the lever was by means of a bearing block that was bolted onto the suspension arm. A second bearing block was bolted onto the bottom tip of each lever. The museum's Firefly has road wheels which are in a good condition. These road wheels were manufactured by various companies in 1943 and 1944. It is believed that these road wheels were exchanged post-war.

Armor PhotoGallery

112 A right side view of museum's Firefly showing the VVSS suspension components. The right side suspension consists only of early spoked type road wheels. All three bogeys have horizontal return roller brackets with raised pillow blocks.

113 Close-up view of the right front bogey.

114 The right drive sprocket. Both drive sprockets are in good condition and have been replaced while in later service.

115 Close-up view of the trailing arm and return roller mount with the bearing pillow block fitted to the right side bogey.

116 The T54E1 track as installed on the right side of the Johannesburg's Firefly. The T54E1 steel track was common on the Sherman series.

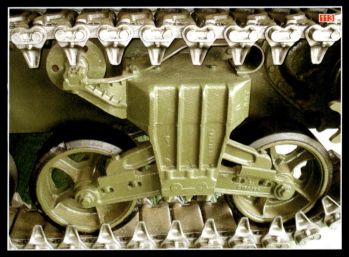

ARMOR PHOTOGALLERY

117 Front view of the museum Firefly. It is armed with a British 17-pdr Mk.VII gun, Barrel No. L/29692, manufactured by the Royal Ordnance Factory in Leeds.

118 The barrel of the QF 17-pdr (76.2 mm) gun is fitted with an egg-shaped muzzle brake with round holes.

119 The left side view of the turret. This is the low bustle, early production, reinforced turret. Note that the turret lacks a pistol port. These were eliminated from turret production in February 1943.

120 121 122 123 Four views of the special 17-pdr gun mantlet. It was different from any other type of Sherman mantlet, notably lacking cheek pieces along the side of the barrel. Note the vertical line of screw heads down the right side of the mount indicating this is the early M34A1 gun mount behind the mantlet.

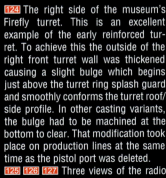

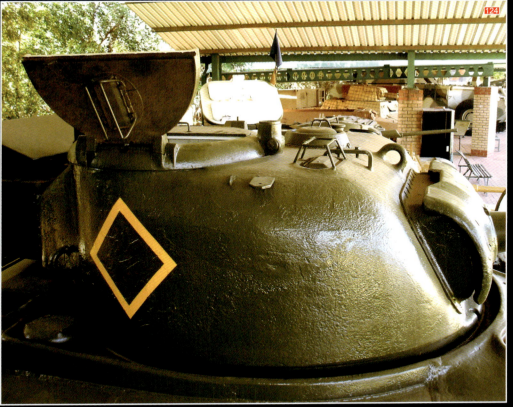

124 The right side of the museum's Firefly turret. This is an excellent example of the early reinforced turret. To achieve this the outside of the right front turret wall was thickened causing a slight bulge which begins just above the turret ring splash guard and smoothly conforms the turret roof/side profile. In other casting variants, the bulge had to be machined at the bottom to clear. That modification took place on production lines at the same time as the pistol port was deleted.

125 126 127 Three views of the radio box. There were two main designs of radio box. In this case, the sides overlapped the rear plate. In the other design, the rear plate overlapped the sides. An additional sponson stowage box was fitted atop the radio box of this vehicle.

128 Overhead view of the sponson stowage box installed on top of the radio box. Note the two antenna mounting points. The „A" aerial for the British No. 19 radio set was installed in the standard socket at the right of the photo, and the „B" aerial was fitted in a small socket to the left of the photo.

129 The left roof of the turret showing the loader's hatch. In Fireflies, an additional hatch for the loader was fitted into the turret roof because of the obstruction caused by the large size of the new gun's breech and recoil guard. The loader's hatch is surrounded with a splash rail.

130 The left roof of the turret showing the loader's rotating M6 periscope. The hole visible in the lower right of the photo indicates that this tank was fitted with the British 2 in. (50.8 mm) bomb thrower in the left front of the turret roof. It was recommended that the bomb thrower be installed in all Shermans as of June 1943, and they first appeared in the early reinforced turrets like this one.

131 The pads on the inside of the loader's hatch. This is the most common type, rectangular with round corners. When open, it was propped up at angle by a large locking catch on the edge of the turret.

132 An overhead view of the left front of the turret showing the loader's hatch and M6 periscope, the turret roof ventilator cover, and the roof fittings for the spotlight. The manufacturer's mark appearing on the ventilator cover denotes the Symington-Gould Corporation, Rochester, NY, and the part number is D86764.

133 An overhead view of the right front of the turret showing the front of the commander's hatch, the gunner's M4 periscope and the turret roof ventilator cover. The mounting base for the improved vane sight (called an Alidade Sight by the British) is visible to the left of the M4 periscope.

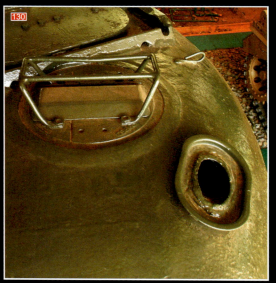

134 View of the commander's split hatch. This is the second design, fitted with counterbalancing springs. The counterbalance design evolved in order to facilitate opening and closing the heavy hatch covers. The lever on the side of the MG pintle socket is used to secure the pintle into the socket.

135 136 The two parts of the commander's split hatch. The sequential part numbers of the hatch covers are D69991 (left) and D69992 (right). This hatch design relied on an external lever operating a spring loaded plunger and was combined with the hatch ring, drawing number D69993. The commander's rotating M6 periscope was normally installed in one of the hatches.

137 The gunner's M4 periscope. The sun compass bracket is welded to the right of the turret roof (extreme left in the photo). .

138 The outside surface of the split hatch that was fitted with the rotating M6 periscope. Note the part number, D69991, and the manufacturer's mark which denotes the Symington-Gould Corporation, Rochester, NY.

139 Close-up view of the commander hatch's counterbalancing spring.

Armor PhotoGallery

140 The inside of the left front turret roof showing the turret roof ventilator mount, the internal 17-pdr gun travel lock, the loader's hatch and the loader's periscope mount.

141 The 0.30 cal. (7.62 mm) Browning M1919A4 co-axial machine gun mount to the left of the 17-pdr gun mount.

142 The loader's hatch in the turret roof.

143 The main gun ammunition ready rack located on the turret floor in front of the loader.

144 The loader's rotating M6 periscope mount and the 2 in. (50.8 mm) bomb thrower mount, incorporated in the front left turret roof.

145 The gunner's side of the turret showing the controls that operate the turret and fire the guns. The telescopic sight is missing.

146 Close-up view of the 17-pdr's right recoil cylinder and the M38 telescope mount.

147 The gunner's M4 periscope mount in the turret roof's front right corner and the M38 telescope mount in the right side of the gun mount.

ARMOR PhotoGallery

145

148 The rear of the breech block. The 17-pdr gun was fitted with a semi-automatic, horizontal, sliding breech block. The 17-pdr fired fixed (one-piece) ammunition including Super Velocity Discarding Sabot (SVDS), also referred to as Armor Piercing, Discarding Sabot (APDS), Armor Piercing, Capped (APC), High Explosive (HE) and Armor Piercing, Capped, Ballistic Capped (APCBC). By D-Day, the most effective 17-pdr armor piercing ammunition was the APCBC solid shot. The new SVDS rounds became available in August 1944. The muzzle velocity was 1200 m/s, and the carrier separated from the core after leaving the muzzle. The SVSD could penetrate homogenous armor plate 193 mm thick, sloped at 30 degrees, at 900 m range (versus 130 mm thick armor for APCBC solid shot).

149 The right wall of the turret. The gunner's M4 periscope mount appears in the upper left of the photo.

146

147

148

149

Armor PhotoGallery

150 The commander's side of the turret immediately under the commander's hatch. Note the slope of the bustle roof typical for low bustle Sherman turrets. The signal pistol was stored on the turret wall immediately below the hatch.

151 Close-up view of the rack for 0.50 cal. (12.7 mm) ammunition boxes.

152 The interior of the radio box fitted to the rear turret. The radio set is missing from this particular vehicle. The first aid box bracket is mounted on the turret ring under the radio box.

153 The rear right corner of the fighting compartment. The engine oil cooler is mounted on the bulkhead. The commander's folding and elevating seat is to the left. Note the L-shaped turret basket support connected to the turret ring.

154 The engine bulkhead. The four handwheels are the fuel shut-off control valves. These are located above the transmission oil cooler air duct.

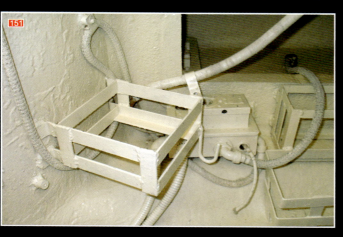

ARMOR PhotoGallery

R975 Engine

155 A Continental R975 engine preserved at the National Museum of Military History in Johannesburg, South Africa. This photo shows the cowling, the flywheel assembly and the engine radiator fan. The R975 engine was a direct descendant of the Lawrance J-1, a nine-cylinder air-cooled radial built by the Lawrance Aero Engine Company for the U.S. Navy. Built by Continental Motors under license from Wright, the R975 delivered 400 hp. With a lower compression ratio than the aero-engine it could run on 80-octane petrol. Being air-cooled, the R975 was lighter and more reliable than a liquid-cooled engine of similar power.

156 An overhead view of the R975 engine, showing its cowling and the exhaust manifold.

157 The top of the engine, showing the cylinder head covers.

158 A close-up view of the front of the engine, showing the motor cranking assembly located between two magnetos, and the engine mounting frame.

Ammunition & Cases

[Right] The 17-pounder ammunition used in Sherman Firefly:
1 – HE/T Mk I: high explosive with tracer;
2 – HE/T Mk II: high explosive with tracer;
3 – HE/T/HC: high capacity high explosive with tracer;
4 – HE/HC Super Mk I;
5 – Solid Armor Piercing Shot;
6 – Armor Piercing Capped;
7 – Armor Piercing Capped; Ballistic Capped;
8 – Armor Piercing Practice;
9 – Armor Piercing Discarding Sabot.

[Below] The 17-pounder ammunition cases: A – 17-pdr Ammunition Case C274 Mk I (wood) containing 2 rounds of A.P., A.P.C., H.E. or Practice (yellow band denotes); B – 17-pdr Ammunition Case C310 Mk I (wood) containing 2 rounds of A.P.C.B.C.; C – 17-pdr Ammunition Case C288 Mk I (steel) containing 2 rounds of A.P., H.E., A.P.C. or A.P.D.S.; D – 17-pdr Ammunition Case C317 Mk I (steel) containing 2 rounds of A.P.C.B.C.

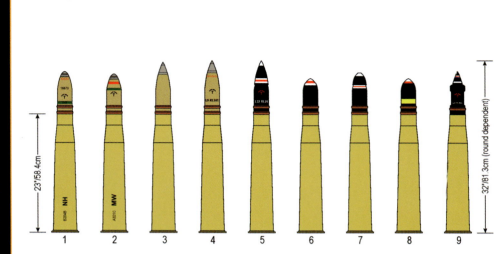

1/17.5 Scale © Barry Beldam

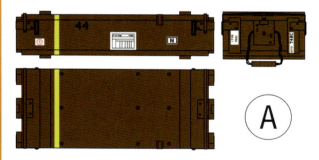

Note: markings are typical and not all inclusive, and boxes came in a number of colors green.

1/17.5 Scale © Barry Beldam

Drawings

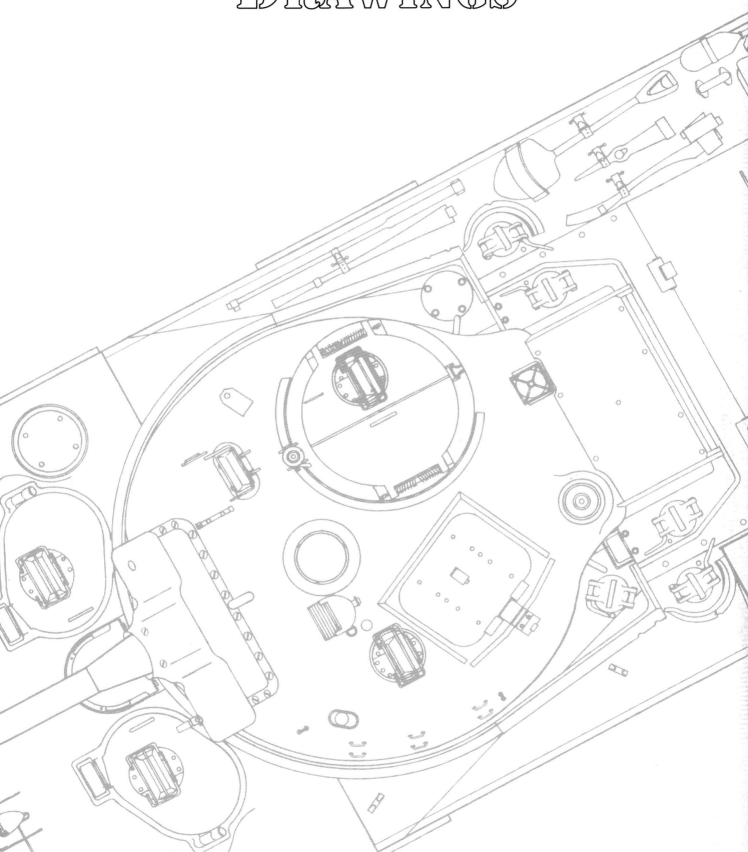

Sherman IC Firefly

Sherman IC Firefly

1/48th Scale

All Round Vision Cupola No.1 Mk.II
1/48th Scale

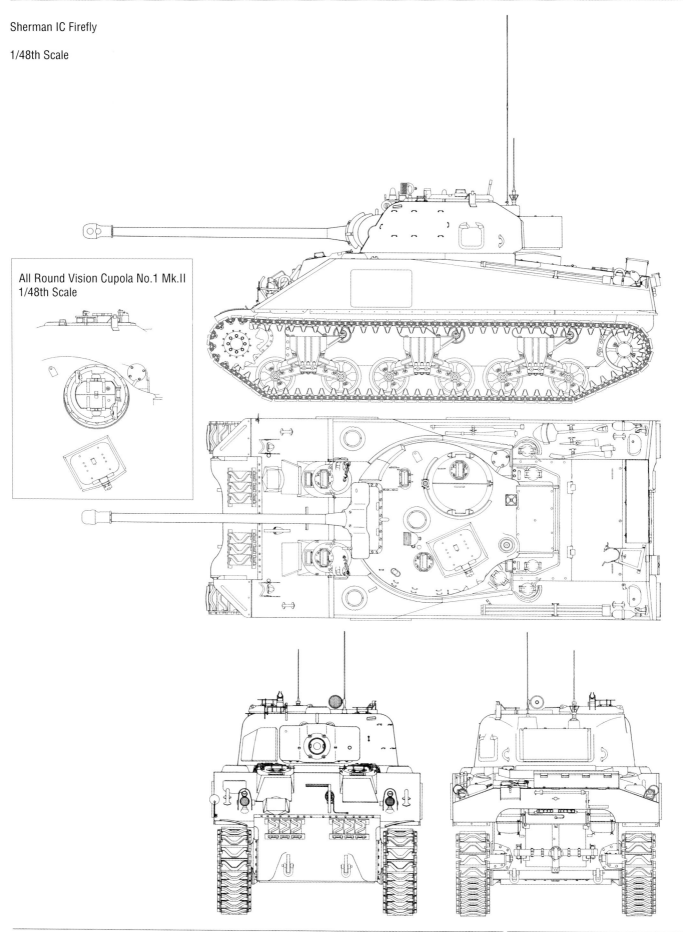

Sherman Hybrid IC Firefly

1/48th Scale

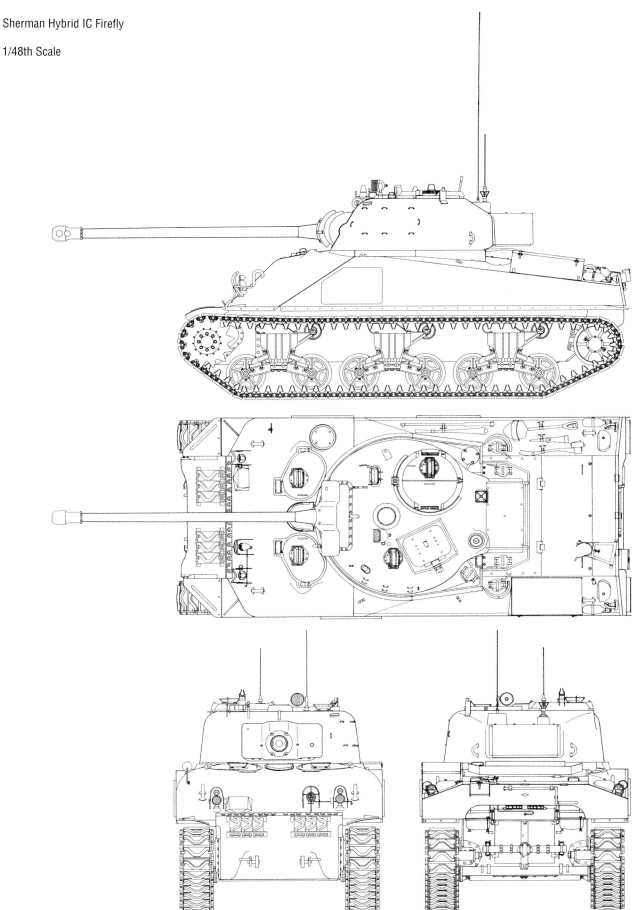

Sherman IC Firefly

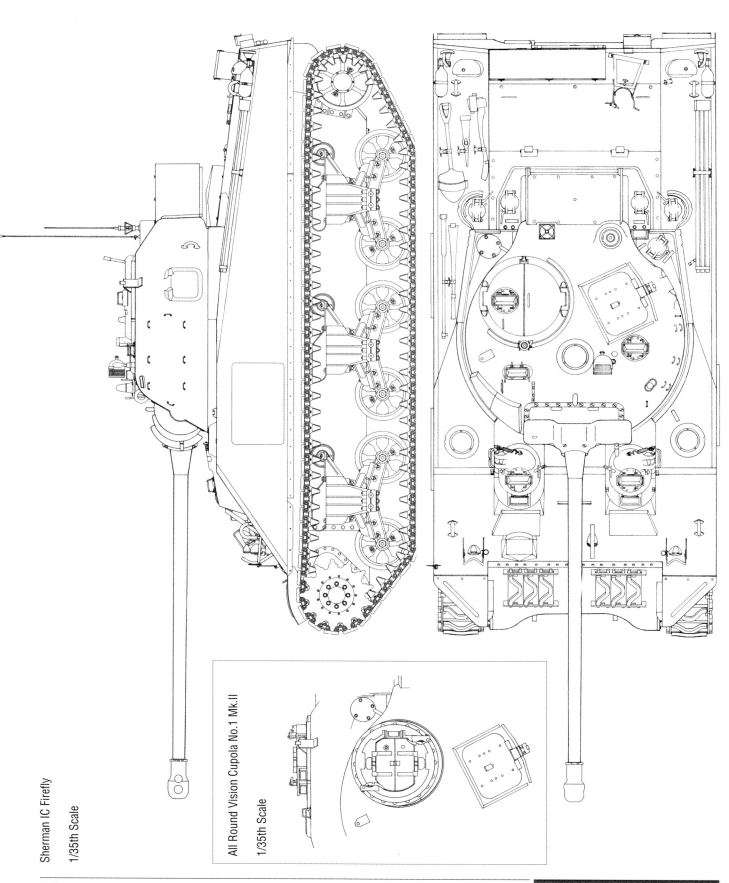

Sherman IC Firefly
1/35th Scale

All Round Vision Cupola No.1 Mk.II
1/35th Scale

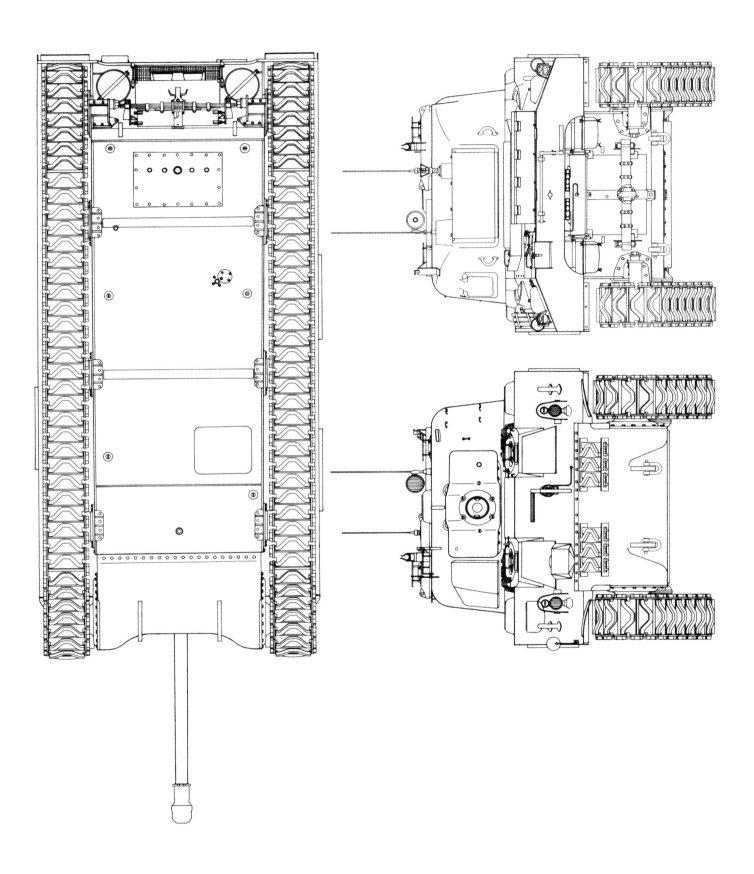

Armor PhotoGallery

Sherman IC Firefly

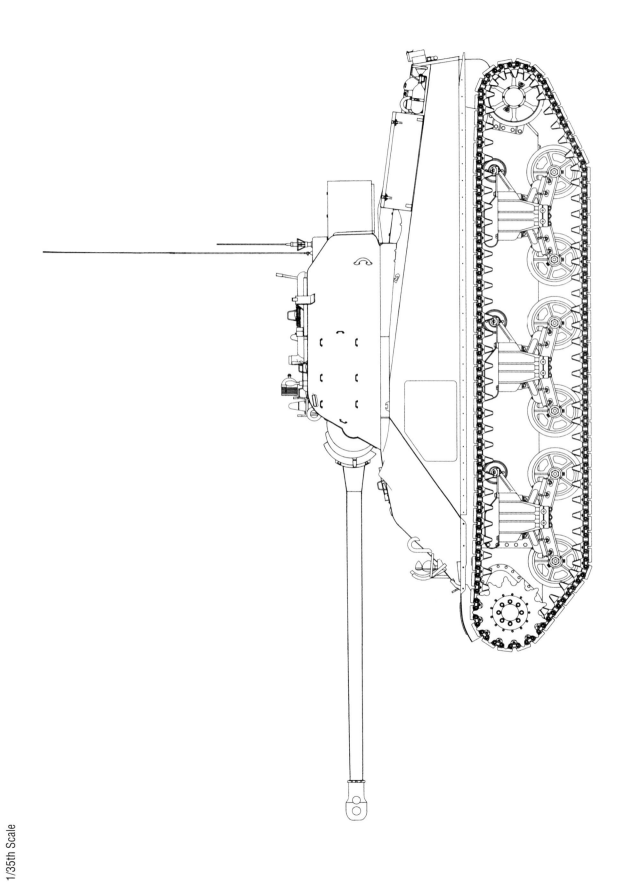

Sherman Hybrid IC Firefly
1/35th Scale

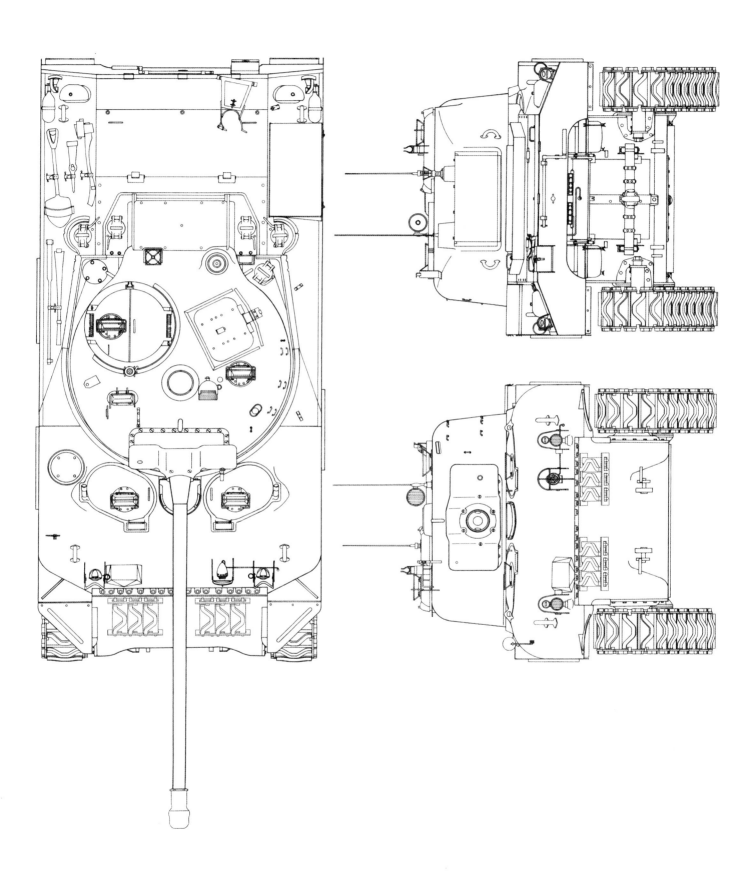

SHERMAN IC FIREFLY

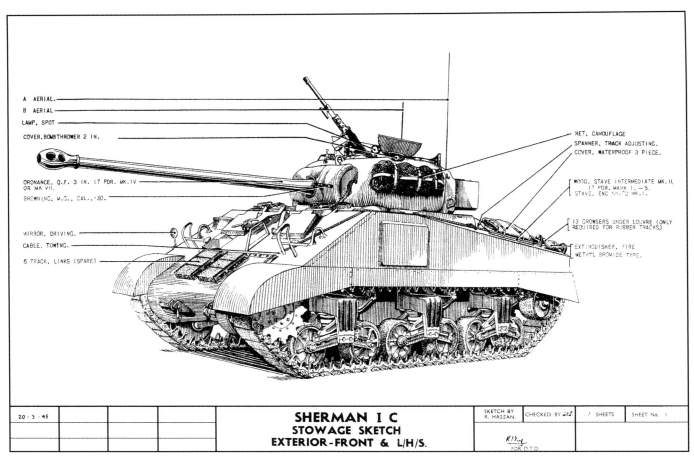

SHERMAN I C
STOWAGE SKETCH
EXTERIOR – FRONT & L/H/S

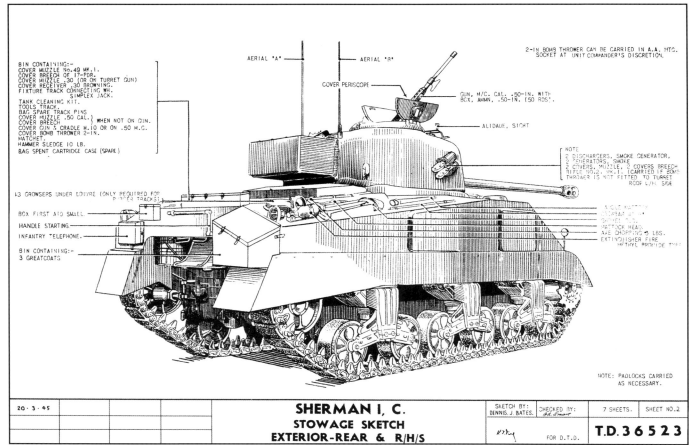

SHERMAN I, C.
STOWAGE SKETCH
EXTERIOR – REAR & R/H/S

T.D. 36523

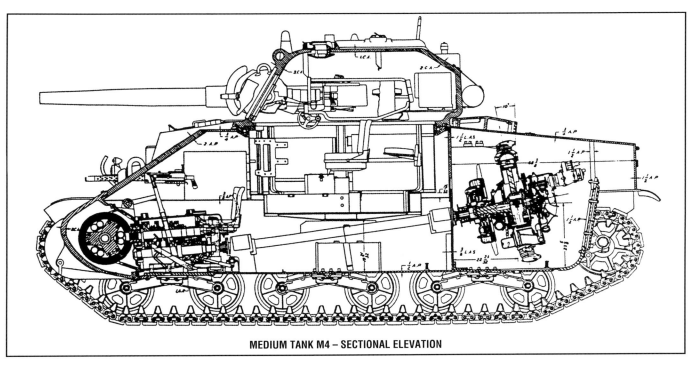

MEDIUM TANK M4 – SECTIONAL ELEVATION

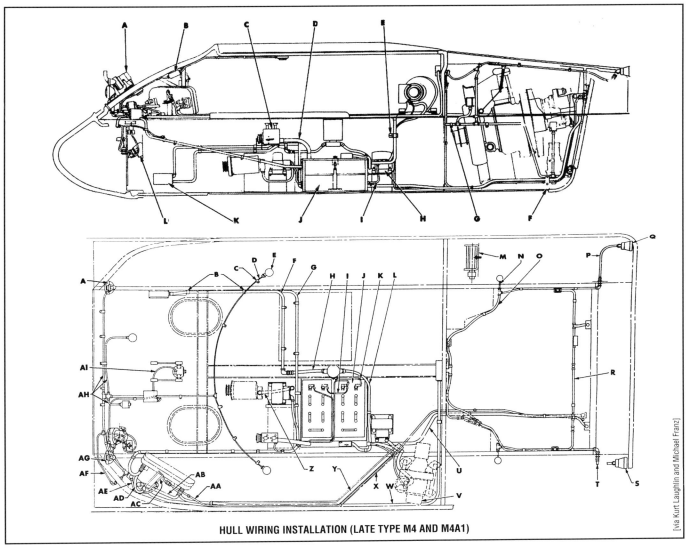

HULL WIRING INSTALLATION (LATE TYPE M4 AND M4A1)

[via Kurt Laughlin and Michael Franz]

43

Sherman IC Firefly

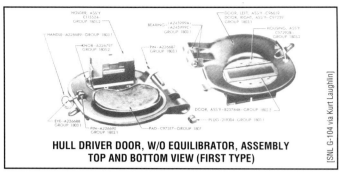

HULL DRIVER DOOR, W/O EQUILIBRATOR, ASSEMBLY TOP AND BOTTOM VIEW (FIRST TYPE)

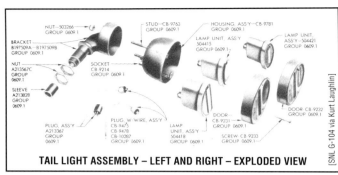

TAIL LIGHT ASSEMBLY – LEFT AND RIGHT – EXPLODED VIEW

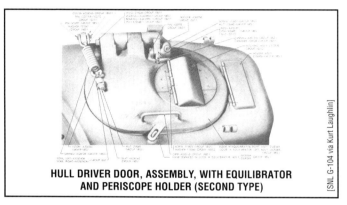

HULL DRIVER DOOR, ASSEMBLY, WITH EQUILIBRATOR AND PERISCOPE HOLDER (SECOND TYPE)

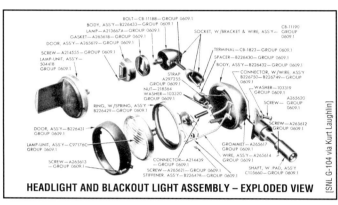

HEADLIGHT AND BLACKOUT LIGHT ASSEMBLY – EXPLODED VIEW

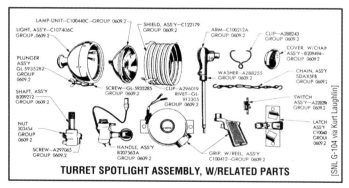

TURRET SPOTLIGHT ASSEMBLY, W/RELATED PARTS

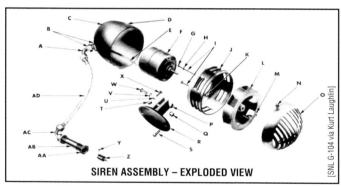

SIREN ASSEMBLY – EXPLODED VIEW

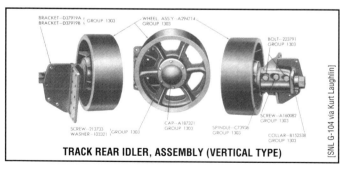

TRACK REAR IDLER, ASSEMBLY (VERTICAL TYPE)

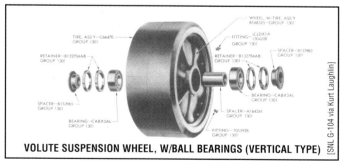

VOLUTE SUSPENSION WHEEL, W/BALL BEARINGS (VERTICAL TYPE)

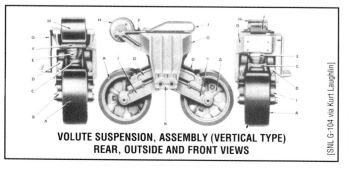

VOLUTE SUSPENSION, ASSEMBLY (VERTICAL TYPE) REAR, OUTSIDE AND FRONT VIEWS

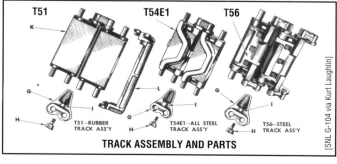

TRACK ASSEMBLY AND PARTS

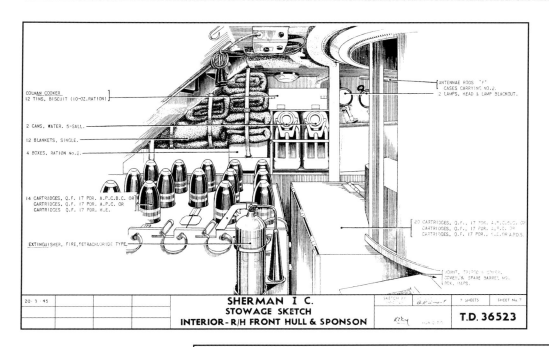

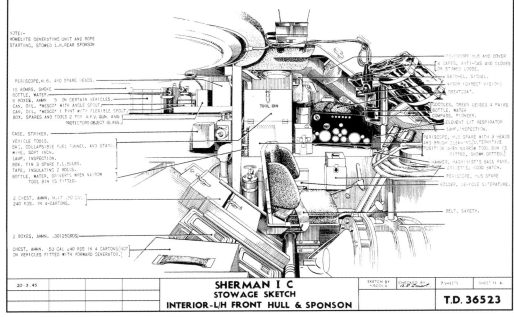

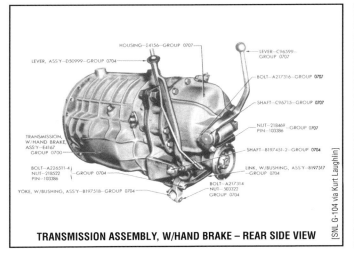

TRANSMISSION ASSEMBLY, W/HAND BRAKE – REAR SIDE VIEW

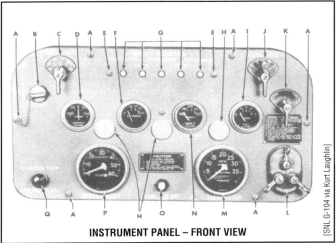

INSTRUMENT PANEL – FRONT VIEW

Sherman IC Firefly

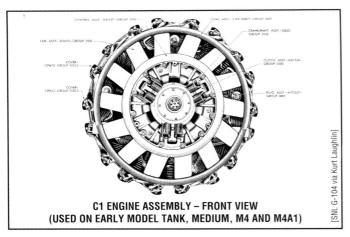

C1 ENGINE ASSEMBLY – FRONT VIEW
(USED ON EARLY MODEL TANK, MEDIUM, M4 AND M4A1)

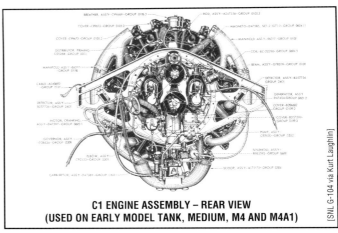

C1 ENGINE ASSEMBLY – REAR VIEW
(USED ON EARLY MODEL TANK, MEDIUM, M4 AND M4A1)

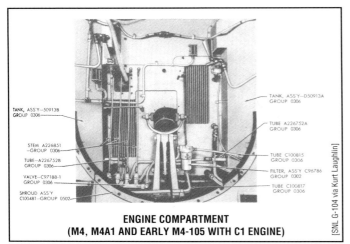

ENGINE COMPARTMENT
(M4, M4A1 AND EARLY M4-105 WITH C1 ENGINE)

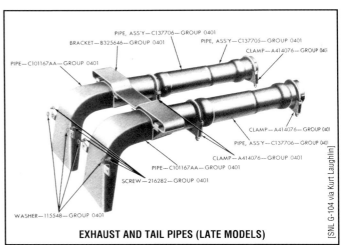

EXHAUST AND TAIL PIPES (LATE MODELS)

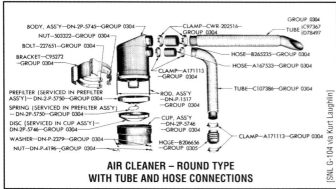

AIR CLEANER – ROUND TYPE
WITH TUBE AND HOSE CONNECTIONS

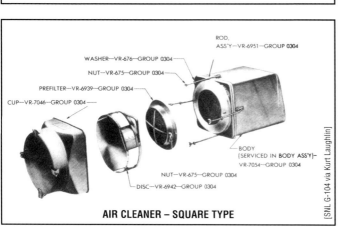

AIR CLEANER – SQUARE TYPE

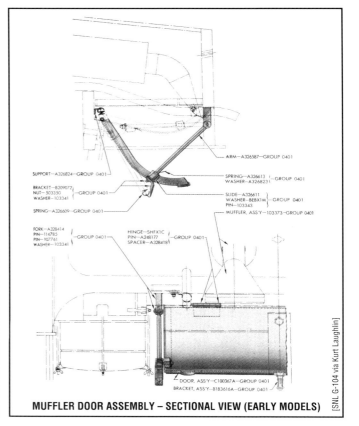

MUFFLER DOOR ASSEMBLY – SECTIONAL VIEW (EARLY MODELS)

BRITISH ALL ROUND VISION CUPOLA NO.1 MK.II – CLOSED

BRITISH ALL ROUND VISION CUPOLA NO.1 MK.II – OPEN

BRITISH ALL ROUND VISION CUPOLA NO.1 MK.II – REAR VIEW

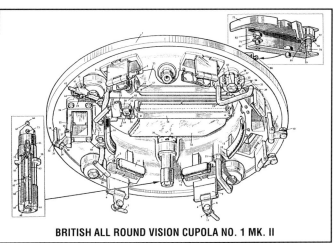
BRITISH ALL ROUND VISION CUPOLA NO. 1 MK. II

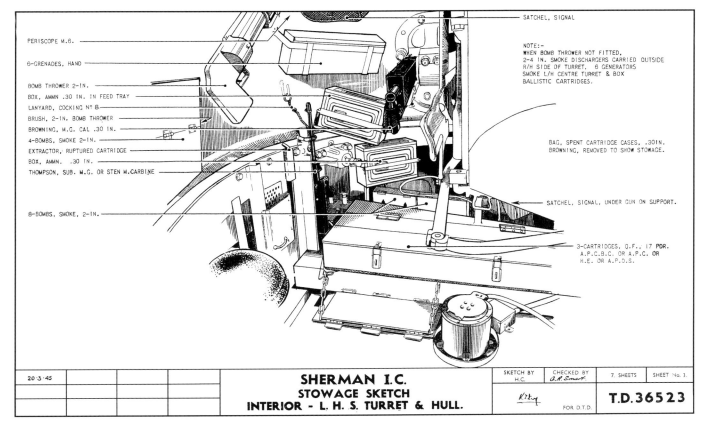

Labels (left side):
- PERISCOPE M.6.
- 6-GRENADES, HAND
- BOMB THROWER 2-IN.
- BOX, AMMN. .30 IN. IN FEED TRAY
- LANYARD, COCKING No 8
- BRUSH, 2-IN. BOMB THROWER
- BROWNING, M.G. CAL .30 IN.
- 4-BOMBS, SMOKE 2-IN.
- EXTRACTOR, RUPTURED CARTRIDGE
- BOX, AMMN. .30 IN.
- THOMPSON, SUB. M.G. OR STEN M. CARBINE
- 8-BOMBS, SMOKE, 2-IN.

Labels (right side):
- SATCHEL, SIGNAL
- NOTE:- WHEN BOMB THROWER NOT FITTED, 2-4 IN. SMOKE DISCHARGERS CARRIED OUTSIDE R/H SIDE OF TURRET, 6 GENERATORS SMOKE L/H CENTRE TURRET & BOX BALLISTIC CARTRIDGES.
- BAG, SPENT CARTRIDGE CASES, .30IN. BROWNING, REMOVED TO SHOW STOWAGE.
- SATCHEL, SIGNAL, UNDER GUN ON SUPPORT.
- 3-CARTRIDGES, Q.F., 17 PDR. A.P.C.B.C. OR A.P.C. OR H.E. OR A.P.D.S.

SHERMAN I.C.
STOWAGE SKETCH
INTERIOR – L.H.S. TURRET & HULL.

Date: 20·3·45 | Sketch by H.C. | Checked by G.R. Smart | 7 SHEETS | SHEET No. 3 | T.D. 36523

SHERMAN IC FIREFLY

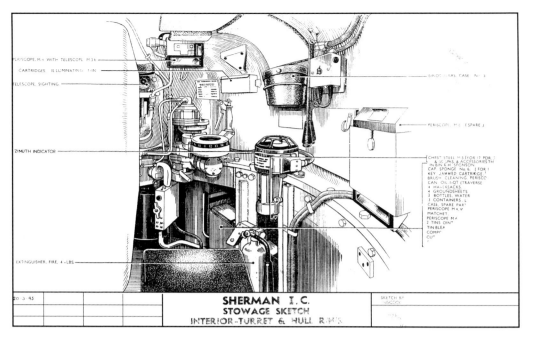

SHERMAN I.C. STOWAGE SKETCH — INTERIOR-TURRET & HULL R.H.S

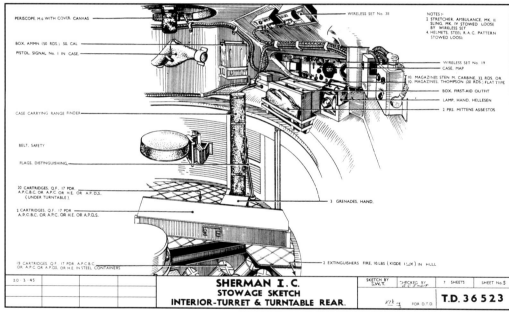

SHERMAN I.C. STOWAGE SKETCH — INTERIOR-TURRET & TURNTABLE REAR — T.D. 36523

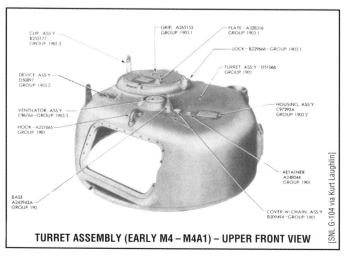

TURRET ASSEMBLY (EARLY M4 – M4A1) – UPPER FRONT VIEW

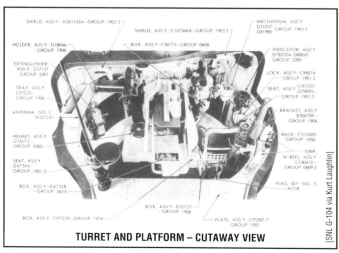

TURRET AND PLATFORM – CUTAWAY VIEW

PhotoHistory

The Firefly was the most successful British modification to the American Sherman tank and was the result of rearming U.S.-supplied M4 series medium tanks with the British 17-pdr high velocity anti-tank gun. Initially, all 17-pdr conversions were to be on M4A4 Sherman V chassis. Due to a shortage in the numbers of available M4A4 Shermans, by the summer of 1944 more and more M4 and M4 Hybrid Shermans were being converted to Fireflies. By the end of war, the Firefly IC based on the M4 Sherman I and M4 Sherman I Hybrid outnumbered the Sherman VC in most British, Canadian, Polish and Czechoslovakian armored units in North-West Europe.

The Firefly

To be converted into Fireflies, a Sherman tank was required to include the following features: wide mantlet, M34A1 gun mount, petrol driven engine, and hydraulic traverse. These criteria, coupled with vehicle availability, meant that Fireflies were produced primarily on M4A4 and later production M4 tanks. Technically speaking, it was the project to convert the Sherman to accept the 17-pdr that was called the Firefly, the vehicle name did not change. A Sherman I retrofitted with the 17-pdr became a Sherman IC. Notwithstanding this, the converted Shermans were generally known as Fireflies so the Sherman IC was known as the Firefly IC.

A large number of the Sherman ICs were made using the late production Composite hull. This hull incorporated a cast upper front hull welded to the remainder of the hull which was fabricated from welded plates. In Commonwealth service, this variant was called Sherman I Hybrid and thus the 17-pdr versions were Firefly IC Hybrids.

[Continued on page 63]

[Top] En route to the Zuider Zee, this Sherman IC Hybrid of the 8th Princess Louise's (New Brunswick) Hussars of the 5th Canadian Armored Division, moves through Putten in the Netherlands on 18 April 1945. The tank is covered with Churchill track, while a false muzzle brake is fitted halfway along the gun barrel. The rest of the barrel is painted in a counter-shaded pattern. The unit's white 52 can just be seen behind the spare track on the final drive cover. [PA131043 via Barry Beldam]

Sherman IC Firefly

[All photos, this page] Four views of the Sherman IC Firefly (T-263482) belonging to the Mechanical Experimental Establishment – the MEE's triangular symbol can be seen painted on the hull sides. The vehicle is fitted with the open-spoke road wheels and the rear upper hull plate is vertical – both common features on initial production M4s. The metal strip guard for the siren, mounted on the glacis, is typical for remanufactured M4s. [Tank Museum]

[Right] A column of Allied transport passing through Putanges (14 km south-east of Falaise) on 20 August 1944. A Sherman IC appears in the background of the photo. [Daniele Guglielmi Collection]

[Above left] A Hybrid IC Firefly tank of 2nd Irish Guards, Guards Armored Division, near Beauvais, north of Paris, on 31 August 1944. [Photograph BU302 courtesy of the Imperial War Museum, London]

[Above] A Sherman Hybrid IC Firefly (T-263176) advances towards Aunay-sur-Odon, 31 July – 1 August 1944. Note the Sherman V type stowage box fitted to the glacis. [Photograph B8370 courtesy of the Imperial War Museum, London]

[Left] A Sherman Hybrid IC Firefly with other vehicles on the square of the village of Putanges, Normandy, on 20 August 1944. This tank probably belonged to the 23rd Hussars, 29th Armored Brigade, 11th Armored Division. [Photograph B9477 courtesy of the Imperial War Museum, London]

Sherman IC Firefly

[Left] A Sherman Hybrid IC of the 7th Armored Division near Stadtlohn, Germany, on 31 March 1945. [Photograph BU2890 courtesy of the Imperial War Museum, London]

[Right] This column of British Sherman tanks – including at least two ICs – probably belong to the British 33rd Armored Brigade. These were probably photographed at Hotton on 5 January 1945, as the Brigade moved to counterattack during the Ardennes Offensive. [Tank Museum]

[Far right] Sherman tanks of 11th Armored Division during the advance towards Gemert, 26 September 1944. The vehicle in the foreground is a Firefly Hybrid IC. [Tank Museum]

[Right] Shermans of the Guards Armored Division passing by the 1914-1918 Australian Memorial near Villers-Bretonneux, France, on 1 September 1944. A Hybrid IC (T-2634570) of the 2nd Armored Battalion, Coldstream Guards is nearest to the camera. [Photograph BU271 courtesy of the Imperial War Museum, London]

[Left] The Sherman Hybrid IC Firefly "Crazy-Gang", named after a then popular group of English music hall comedians. The vehicle has a stowage box fitted to the rear of the radio box, the rear section of the sand shields is welded to the top of the sponson, and the barrel is counter-shaded. [Tank Museum]

[Right] Tanks of the 8th Armored Brigade in Alpen near Geldern, Germany, on 11 March 1945. The tank nearest camera is a IC Firefly, showing the late production exhaust deflector grill and the stowage bin located across the rear engine deck. [Photograph B15535 courtesy of the Imperial War Museum, London]

Sherman IC Firefly

[Right] A Sherman Hybrid IC driving through Geldern, Germany, on 6 March 1945. [Photograph B15229 courtesy of the Imperial War Museum, London]

[Below] An overhead view of a Sherman Hybrid IC on the Wessel Road, leading out of Geldern, south-east of Kevalaer, on 6 March 1945. Note the extensive stowage carried on the deck plate. [Photograph B15230 courtesy of the Imperial War Museum, London]

[Left] Sherman IC and other vehicles of the 1st Royal Tank Regiment, 22nd Armored Brigade, 7th Armored Division in Ahaus, Germany, on 1 April 1945. [Photograph BU3135 courtesy of the Imperial War Museum, London]

[Below] Canadian Sherman tanks, including a Firefly IC in the foreground, being used as artillery, somewhere in Germany, towards the end of the war. Note the appliqué armor plates fitted to both the hull and turret of the Firefly. [Tank Museum]

[Bottom] A column of Sherman tanks of the 1st Coldstream Guards, British Guards Armored Division, firing at enemy positions in a wood in Bergandlusche on the outskirts of Bremen during the advance into Germany, on 12 April 1945. All the tanks in the column are fitted with launching rails for 60 lb. Typhoon rockets. The markings on rear upper hull plate of the Sherman IC Firefly in the foreground indicate that it belonged to C Squadron, 3rd Troop. [Photograph BU3584 courtesy of the Imperial War Museum, London]

Sherman IC Firefly

[*Right*] A Sherman Hybrid IC burns on the side of the road to Ruurlo in the Netherlands, near the German border, on 2 April 1945. [Tank Museum]

[*Below*] Two Sherman tanks of the Royal Scots Greys, 4th Armored Brigade, surrounded by abandoned German transport, in Wismar on the Baltic Coast, on 4 May 1945. "Priority", the vehicle nearest the camera, is a Sherman Hybrid IC Firefly. Behind it is a Sherman Hybrid I armed with a 75 mm gun. The Firefly has a mix of solid plain disc and pressed spoke type road wheels. [Photograph BU5308 courtesy of the Imperial War Museum, London]

[Above] A IC or Hybrid IC of the British 4th Armored Brigade crosses the River Aller at Rethem, south-east of Bremen, on 16 April 1945. Note the Sherman V-style stowage box fitted to the rear of the turret's radio box. [Photograph BU3649 courtesy of the Imperial War Museum, London]

[Left] Sherman Hybrid IC Firefly of the 7th Armored Division crossing the Kaiser Wilhelm Canal near Steenfeld, on 9 May 1945. The turret has been reversed and the barrel secured by its gun travel lock. [Photograph BU6131 courtesy of the Imperial War Museum, London]

[Left] Two Sherman tanks, probably from representative detachments of the 8th Armored Brigade, taking part in the Victory Parade of the 51st Highland Division, through Bremershaven on 12 May 1945. The salute was taken by Lieutenant-General Horrocks, commander of the XXX Corps. The vehicle on the left is a Sherman Hybrid IC. [Photograph BU6114 courtesy of the Imperial War Museum, London]

Sherman IC Firefly

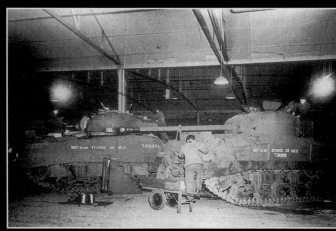

[Far left] A group of three Sherman Hybrid IC Fireflies, undergoing waterproofing for a sea journey, at the tank depot at Chilwell, Nottinghamshire, U.K. These tanks were probably destined for Italy. The tank in the center, T-269782, has the typical long stowage box (with its hinges to the rear), and a first aid box fitted to the rear hull plate. The turret pistol port is absent, while the towing hook for a 17-pdr anti-tank gun is visible on the floor. [Tank Museum]

[Left] Two Sherman Hybrid IC Fireflies being waterproofed at Chilwell. The left tank is T-269782, while the similar tank to the right has the serial number T-269802. [Tank Museum]

[Left] A IC Hybrid in Italy crossing the Bando Canal, between Ferrara and Bologna on 12 April 1945. The broken span has bridged by a Churchill ARK tank. [Photograph NA24139 courtesy of the Imperial War Museum, London]

[Above] A Sherman Hybrid IC using the cover of buildings, while preparing to fire on enemy positions along the banks of the River Reno, Italy, on 6 April 1945. The tank fire was to support an assault crossing by C Company, 1st Battalion, London Irish Rifles. The rear of the tank's turret displays a large B Squadron identification sign. The track extensions are made of T-section angle iron. [Photograph NA23754 courtesy of the Imperial War Museum, London]

[Left] A heavily camouflaged Sherman Hybrid IC tank crosses a Bailey bridge over the River Santerno near Imola, Italy, on 12 April 1945. To conceal the 17-pdr gun, a tin can has been placed half way along the barrel, with a counter-shaded camouflage paint scheme on one side and hessian wrapping on the other. [Photograph NA24026 courtesy of the Imperial War Museum, London]

Sherman IC Firefly

[Above & right] Two photos showing Canadian Sherman IC Fireflies belonging to the Fort Garry Horse, 2nd Canadian Armored Brigade, at a cross-roads near the Beveland Canal on 29 October 1944. [Tank Museum & Zbigniew Lalak Collection]

[Above right] A Sherman Hybrid IC Firefly of the 2nd Canadian Armored Brigade's Sherbrooke Fusiliers Regiment, in the Netherlands, in late 1944. Note the extra track, fitted as auxiliary armor, as well as the crew's RAC Mk.I steel helmets, slung along the side of the turret. [Public Archives of Canada via Berry Beldam]

[Below] A very interesting shot of a Sherman IC of the Fort Garry Horse, 2nd Canadian Armored Brigade, in Germany, on 25 April 1945. Log armor was extensively used by the FGH and several other units as one of the many expedients to provide additional protection against the ubiquitous Panzerfaust, which was able penetrate up to 200 mm of armor and caused, by this stage of the War, a third of all allied tank losses. Tests by First Canadian Army showed that none of these expedients were particularly effective. [PA166803 via Berry Beldam]

[Left] A Sherman IC Hybrid of the South Alberta Regiment (the armored recce regiment of the 4th Canadian Armored Division) plods along through the wet lowlands of the Hochwald near Calcar on 26 February 1945. Like many tanks towards the war's end the outside looks like a disaster area but provides for all the diverse needs of the crew. [PA113675 via Berry Beldam]

[Below left] A Canadian Sherman IC Hybrid. The vehicle has only its serial number visible (T-263652) plus some white chalked numbers. The front hull is covered with extra track, including at least one underneath going the other way. It appears that the censor has covered the formation sign on the one-piece differential housing and there is no any unit sign. Note that the usual stains from spilt fuel are plainly evident. Note the usual position of the commander in the turret, with the hatch doors open and his head as low as possible, to try to provide a poor target for snipers. [DND Army S-0043pc via Steve Guthrie]

[Below] Three late-war Canadian Shermans moving along a road behind the fighting, with a Hybrid IC leading the column. Despite the lack of any markings, this photo shows the "typical" Sherman of the time, covered with spare track and wearing extension grousers. The place is probably in the Netherlands, towards the end of the war. The second tank has no track on the hull sides whereas the other two do. [DND Army S-0078p via Steve Guthrie]

[Left] A pair of Sherman ICs trundle past the infantry to get to their job somewhere in the Netherlands, in 1945. These tanks fit the usual pattern for this unit (The Fort Garry Horse), at this place and this time; the "horse hair" covered turret and hull and the heavily laden rear hulls with many used ammunition boxes for stowage. Just to the right of the phone box, on the left edge of the rear hull plate, a very faint 52 on a dark colored rectangle, with a white stripe underneath, can be seen. A small circle in the dead center of the rear hull plate, possibly indicates that this is a C Squadron vehicle. [DND Army 0021p via Steve Guthrie]

Sherman IC Firefly

[Above] A long row of Shermans, including two Fireflies, rest along the main road of a small village, near the end of the war. The closest vehicle is a Sherman IC, possibly a Hybrid, named "Beast III". On the left side of the rear hull the left upper corner of the unit sign is visible. The two visible numbers "17" indicate the 1st Canadian Armored Brigade. From the shape of the crews' cap badges, they could belong to the Ontario Regiment. All the tanks have extra track as auxiliary armor and are covered by recently-cut conifer branches. Extension grousers are also evident all along the line. [DND Army 0156p via Steve Guthrie]

[Right] This Sherman IC Hybrid sits menacingly in front of a bomb damaged building, probably in the Netherlands, on 11 April 1945. The gun has been partially covered with mesh to break up its outline and there is a eight-barreled smoke grenade discharger mounted on the turret behind the mantlet. Near the end of the war these grenade dischargers appeared on many Canadian Army vehicles. Identification of the tank's unit is difficult, as it is not known which formation it belongs to. [DND Army S-49827 via Steve Guthrie]

[Continued from page 49]
Medium tank M4
The basis for the Sherman IC Firefly conversions were M4 Medium tanks, armed with the 75 mm gun and powered by the Continental R975 C1 radial engine. The M4 was the first welded hull production variant of medium tank M4. Its production started in July 1942 at the Pressed Steel Car Company, six months after the start of M4A1 production, and was finished in August 1943. Other manufacturers were soon brought into the production stream. M4 production started at Baldwin Locomotive Works in January 1943 and was phased out in August 1943. M4s were also manufactured at American Locomotive Company from February to December 1943, at Pullman Standard Car Company from May to September 1943, and at Detroit Tank Arsenal from August 1943 to January 1945. A total of 6,748 M4s were produced with the 75 mm gun of which

[Top] The tanks of the Polish 2nd "Warsaw" Armored Division massed for the Loreto parade on 15 August 1945. The photo shows the tanks belonging to the all-Firefly-equipped platoon of the 2nd Squadron, 1st Krechowiecki Lancers. The Sherman IC "Rycerz I" ("Knight I", T-270012) appears in the foreground, while the remaining platoon's three tanks are all Hybrid ICs. The 2nd Armored Division was expanded from the 2nd Armored Brigade on 7 June 1945. [PISM]

[Left] The right side of the Sherman IC Firefly "Rycerz I". The leading tank is the Sherman III "Rozmach I" ("Impetus I"). Note "Rycerz I" is fitted with the British All Round Vision cupola. [PISM]

Sherman IC Firefly

2,096 were shipped to the British through Lend-Lease.
The construction of late production M4s built at the Detroit Tank Arsenal differed in having upper front hull consisted of a single armor steel casting, welded to the remainder of the hull which was fabricated, as usual, from rolled plate. The new front full included new, larger drivers' hatches mounted in the roof of the front hull so the drivers' hoods were completely eliminated. These vehicles were sometimes called M4 Composite Hull in the U.S. Army, and Sherman I Hybrid by the British.
From August 1944 to April 1945, 795 M4 tanks were refurbished within the remanufacturing program. This figure includes 446 vehicles rebuilt at Chrysler's Evansville plant, 289 by International Harvester at the Quad Cities Tank Arsenal, and 60 at the Chester and Lima Tank Depots.
Combat experience showed that a considerable number of losses

[Top] Tanks of the 1st Squadron, 1st Krechowiecki Lancers, Polish 2nd Armored Brigade massed for the parade at Loreto, on 15 August 1945, with the three vehicles of the same platoon in the center of the photo: Sherman III "Brawura" ("Bravery", T-149540), Sherman Hybrid IC Firefly "Bestja" ("Beast", T-269793) and Sherman III "Bat" ("Whip"). Tanks of the 2nd Squadron are visible in the right. "Bestja" is fitted with the British All Round Vision cupola. The Loreto Basilica appears in the far background. [PISM]

[Right] A Sherman Hybrid IC Firefly named "Żądło" ("Sting") of 3rd Squadron, 1st Krechowiecki Lancers Armored Regiment during the fighting prior to the capture of Bologna in April 1945. The regimental insignia and the tank's name are yellow while the tactical marking is in white. The radio call code plate is fitted on rear side of the turret over the tactical marking. [PISM]

[Left] Sherman Hybrid IC "Żyrafa" ("Giraffe") of the 3rd Squadron, 1st Krechowiecki Lancers, Polish 2nd Armored Brigade. Polish armored regiments in the MTO followed the British system of tactical markings, introduced in 1940. The regimental HQ squadron used a hollow diamond, the 1st squadron a hollow triangle, the 2nd squadron a hollow square, while the 3rd squadron used a hollow circle. Tactical markings were to be painted on the rear and both sides of the turret. The color of these tactical signs denoted the position of the unit in the brigade. A red tactical sign denoted the senior regiment in the brigade, yellow the second regiment, and blue the junior regiment (in the 2nd Armored Brigade, these were the 4th Armored Regiment, the 1st Krechowiecki Lancers and the 6th Armored Regiment, respectively). Unbrigaded regiments like the Carpathian Lancers carried white tactical signs. [PISM]

[Above left] A Sherman Hybrid IC "Zemsta II" ("Revenge II"; T-269854) of 3rd Squadron, 1st Krechowiecki Lancers drives over a Churchill ARK. The tank commander is sporting a captured helmet. [PISM]

[Above] Sherman Hybrid IC "Bóbr II" ("Beaver II") of the 1st Squadron, 1st Krechowiecki Lancers, Polish 2nd Armored Brigade at the Loreto parade on 15 August 1945. This tank is fitted with the British All Round Vision cupola. [PISM]

[Left] One of a few Sherman ICs issued to the 4th "Scorpion" Armored Regiment, 2nd Armored Brigade during a rest at Potenza-Picena in February/March 1945. The turret of this tank is fitted with the British pattern Mk. II All Round Vision cupola, designed to improve the tank commander's field of view when the tank was closed up. These vision cupolas were issued to a very small number of Fireflies. [PISM]

Sherman IC Firefly

[Right] The Sherman IC Firefly of the 4th Armored Regiment during the pursuit towards Bologna in April 1945. [PISM]

[Bottom] A column of vehicles of the Polish 4th Armored Regiment during postwar exercises in the area of Civita Nuova in Italy early in July 1946. The lead tank, a 75 mm gun Sherman III, is followed by the 17-pdr-armed Sherman IC Firefly. Initially all medium tanks in the Polish 2nd Brigade's armored equipment were the 75 mm Sherman IIIs. While the Brigade was resting in the Potenza-Picena area in the winter of 1944/45, it was issued with a new, more potent, mix of Sherman tanks: 105 mm howitzer-armed Sherman IBs, and 17-pdr gun-armed Sherman ICs and Hybrid ICs. Further Firefly tanks were allocated in the following months, with the 24 vehicles shown in the RAC Progress Report of the 10 February, and 36 vehicles in the Report of the 7 April 1945. [PISM]

resulted from ammunition fires inside the tank. To prevent this, 25 mm thick appliqué armor plates were welded to the outside of the hull to protect the sponson ammunition racks. One plate was placed over the single rack on the left side and a plate was welded over each of the two racks on the right. In order to increase the drivers' protection two 38 mm thick appliqué armor plates were also welded to the front of the drivers' hoods. Both the side and front appliqué armor plates were introduced to production and during modernization as well as being installed as a field modification.

Only the earliest production M4s were fitted with the three-piece bolted differential and final drive housing adapted from the medium tank M3 series. Late production vehicles had the one piece casting: the original model of the rounded profile was fitted with a single anchor brake system while the later model, with the pointed beak, came with double anchor brakes. All M4s used the heavy duty vertical volute spring suspension (VVSS). Initially, the production suspension units mounted to M4s were fitted with the symmetrical track skid design. Mid production vehicles had bogies fitted with the revised skewed shape skid while the bulk of the production vehicles had bogies fitted with final shape skid which made a 180 degree loop before being attached to the bogie bracket casting. During the production run, the return roller was raised to accommodate improved and heavier types of track. Initially, a thicker pillow block was added under the roller axle to raise it. The later version had an upswept arm that accomplished the same thing while simplifying production. It was installed on latest production M4 Hybrids manufactured by Detroit Tank Arsenal.

Most M4s left the factories with road wheels made from stamped
[Continued on page 70]

[Left, below left & below] Three photos of a knocked-out and burned Sherman IC Hybrid "Powab" ("Charm") of the 2nd Squadron, 4th "Scorpion" Armored Regiment. The Sherman was lost from a hit by a Tiger's 8.8 cm round in the fighting preceding the capture of Bologna. Note the remains of the track after the rubber pads have been burned away. [PISM]

[Left] Rear view of another Polish 4th Armored Regiment's Sherman Hybrid IC Firefly knocked-out in the battle for Bologna in April 1945. The photos show almost all features common for the late production Sherman Hybrid IC Firefly. [PISM]

Sherman IC Firefly

[Top] The Loreto parade held on 15 August 1945. The Sherman III Command Tank "Quizil-Ribat" (T-152522) belongs to Gen. Bronisław Rakowski, GOC of the 2nd "Warsaw" Armored Division, who commanded the parade. The Sherman III "Taran" ("Battering-ram") of the 1st Squadron, 4th "Scorpion" Armored Regiment is followed by a Sherman IC Firefly from the same platoon. Note the camouflage applied to the 17-pdr gun barrel. Field Marshal Harold Alexander and Gen. Władysław Anders, commander of the Polish 2nd Corps, review the salute from the platform in the background. [PISM]

[Above] Another scene from the Loreto parade. The Sherman Hybrid IC "Tempo" (T-269761) of the 1st Squadron, 4th "Scorpion" Armored Regiment passes the platform. Note the Sherman III-type stowage box fitted to the radio box. [PISM]

[Left] The platoon of tanks of the 1st Squadron, 4th "Scorpion" Armored Regiment, 2nd Armored Brigade, massed for the Loreto parade; l. to r.: Sherman III, Sherman IC "Trzyniec" (T-331605) and Sherman III "Topór" ("Chopper"). "Trzyniec" is fitted with the British pattern Mk. II vision cupola for the commander and the two 4-inch (102 mm) smoke dischargers mounted on the right side of the turret. The 2nd Armored Brigade followed the widely used British Army system of individual tank names given for tactical purposes. The color and shape of tank names varied greatly during combat operations, but near the end of the war and after the hostilities, the tank names were standardized. In the 4th Armored Regiment characters were red with white shadows. In the HQ Squadron all tank names began with the letter G, in the 1st Squadron – with T, in 2nd Squadron – with P, in 3rd Squadron – with S. In the 1st Krechowiecki Lancers tank names were painted yellow. In the HQ Squadron all tank names began with the letter K, in the 1st Squadron – with B, in the 2nd Squadron – with R, in the 3rd Squadron – with Z. In the 6th Armored Regiment tank names were painted blue. In the HQ Squadron all tank names began with the letter L, in the 1st Squadron – with W, in the 2nd Squadron – with J, in the 3rd Squadron – with M. [PISM]

[Left] Polish Shermans of 1st Squadron, 4th "Scorpion" Armored Regiment of 2nd Armored Brigade, parading on the Loreto airfield, 15 August 1945. A Sherman Hybrid IC with no tactical markings appears in the foreground. [PISM]

[Right] A Hybrid IC "Pawian" ("Baboon") of the 2nd Squadron, 4th "Scorpion" Armored Regiment at the Loreto parade, 15 August 1945. Note the latest production VVSS bogeys fitted with an upswept arm for the return roller, and the British All Round Vision cupola for the commander. [PISM]

[Below] Another photo of Sherman IC "Trzyniec" of the 1st Squadron, 4th "Scorpion" Armored Regiment. The right side of the hull and the left side of the turret are visible on this photo. [PISM]

[Left] The Loreto parade, 15 August 1945. The photo shows in the background the Sherman IC "Sirocco" of the 3rd Squadron, 4th "Scorpion" Armored Regiment, bearing the full array of markings painted on the tanks of the 2nd Armored Brigade in the final days of the war: the name on the hull side and the regimental insignia and the tactical marking on the turret side. All three armored regiments of the 2nd Armored Brigade introduced and used a unique system of regimental insignia, which were painted on both sides of the tank turret, and were usually combined with the tactical markings. The 4th "Scorpion" Armored Regiment introduced a black scorpion, the 1st Krechowiecki Lancers used a horse's head painted in yellow or white, and the 6th "Children of Lvov" Armored Regiment adopted a gold rampant lion, taken from the city crest of Lvov, painted in yellow. [PISM]

Sherman IC Firefly

[Right] The Sherman Hybrid IC "Sztorm" ("Storm") of the 3rd Squadron, 4th "Scorpion" Armored Regiment during the last post-war training exercise at Civita Nuova, Italy, early in July 1946. The tank is fitted with the typical long stowage box, first aid box and the 17-pdr gun travel lock. [PISM]

[Continued from page 66] and embossed steel plate. Some had six embossed spokes and others were of a smooth, dish type further simplifying the design. The original idler wheel was an open spoke design with six spokes. The later idler wheel was the similar to the stamped and spoked road wheel design. The 13-tooth drive sprockets used on Shermans were of three main types. The original sprocket design was cast with various indentations and cutouts to minimize weight, but these were shown to be expensive to manufacture and prone to failure, the second design had a simpler shape without the indentations of the casting and were cut from flat steel plate. The final design was further simplified with a simple, circular hole for the inner diameter and the only finishing being performed on the outer profile.

The early production vehicles were fitted with the M34 combination gun mount which featured the narrow rotor shield. Later in production, the mantlet was redesigned and extended to each side to protect both the new elevation slot for the telescope to the right, and the co-axial machine gun slot to the left. This resulted in the M34A1 combination gun mount which was standardized in October 1942. Still later, the M34A1 gun mount was improved further by having the gun shield thickened across the full width of the mount, and the mantlet was widened on the same side to fit. At the same time, the two lifting eyes welded on the top edge of the rotor shield were replaced with two tapped holes into which lifting eyes could be screwed.

A metal vane sight was introduced in production in the fall of 1942. This sight consisted of the front, larger metal blade welded to the front of the turret roof just to the right of the gunner's periscopic sight, and a shorter blade attached to the turret hatch door in front of the commander's periscope. The metal vane sight was later superseded in production by the improved vane sight (called an Alidade Sight by the British) installed as a single unit on the front of the turret roof to the left of the gun- *[Continued on page 74]*

[Right] New soldiers of the Polish 4th Armored Regiment swear an oath in the front of the Sherman Hybrid IC Firefly. Note the details of the camouflaged end of the 17-pdr gun barrel. [PISM]

[Left] A column of Sherman tanks of the 3rd Squadron, 4th "Scorpion" Armored Regiment grouped for the 4th Regiment's last post-war training exercise at Civita Nuova early in July, 1946. The tank nearest to the camera is the Sherman IC Firefly fitted with the typical long stowage box, first aid box and the gun travel lock. Other tanks visible on the photo include a Sherman Hybrid IC Firefly, another Sherman IC Firefly and two Sherman IIIs. [PISM]

[Left] A column of Polish 4th Armored Regiment's Shermans. The leading Sherman IC shows the configuration of the spare track link brackets on the front hull, and the All Round Vision cupola on the turret roof. [PISM]

[Left] The rear hull of a Polish Sherman Hybrid IC, fitted with the less common round air filters. Note also, the exhaust grille and the towing pintle bracket fitted to some late production Sherman ICs. [PISM]

Sherman IC Firefly

[Right] The parade and banner presentation ceremony to the 6th "Children of Lvov" Armored Regiment, 25 May 1946. "Joasia" ("Jane") is a IC Hybrid from 2nd Squadron. The blue tactical marking with yellow rampant lion inside is typical for 6th Armored Regiment's tanks. Tank's name is blue. [PISM]

[Below] Two interesting Shermans of 1st Squadron, 6th "Children of Lvov" Armored Regiment, at the banner presentation ceremony, 25 May 1946. In the foreground – "Wielki Walc" ("Grand Waltz", a IC Hybrid), in the background – a Sherman III "Włóczęga" ("Vagabond"). "Wielki Walc" is fitted with the late production sharp nosed single piece differential and final drive housing, the turret without the pistol port, and the side stowage box on the left sponson. The 6th Armored Regiment's tactical markings and tank names should be

painted in the regimental color, blue, but – possibly due to movie and propaganda reasons – these were repainted in white for better visibility. Inside the triangle, a rampant gold lion, the crest of the City of Lvov. The vehicle's W.D. Number is also in white. [PISM]

[Above right] A Hybrid IC "Jeż" ("Hedgehog") of the 2nd Squadron, 6th "Children of Lvov" Armored Regiment. The tactical marking and the tank's name are in blue. Like most Polish ICs in MTO, it is fitted with the British All Round Vision cupola. [PISM]

[Right] A relaxed atmosphere is visible in this post-war photo of a Sherman IC of the 6th "Children of Lvov" Armored Regiment stored in the regimental tank depot. Note the counter-shaded camouflage on the barrel, and extensive stowage on the rear hull, including British pattern fire extinguishers and the tank's waterproof cover. [PISM]

[Left & below left] A Hybrid IC "Zamość" (T-268930) of the 1st Squadron, Carpathian Lancers – the recce regiment of the 2nd "Warsaw" Armored Division. The white tactical marking on the turret side is combined with the blue-over-red Polish Cavalry pennon painted inside it. In the Carpathian Lancers, all tank names related to specific themes. The regimental HQ Platoon and the HQ Squadron had names relating to the Regiment's history, in the 1st Squadron the names related to the Polish Cavalry's history, in the 2nd Squadron vehicles were named after atmospheric phenomena, while in the 3rd Squadron they bore the names of Polish regions and historical figures. [PISM]

[Bottom] Sherman IC (T-263113) of the Polish 1st Armored Division damaged by mid-barrel explosion of its round at Zevenbergschen Hoek, Noord-Brabant, the Netherlands. The Polish 1st Armored Division, commanded by Gen. Stanislaw Maczek, was formed in the U.K. on 26 February 1942. During October 1943, the Division was reorganized into its final divisional organization with a single armored brigade. The 10th Armored Cavalry Brigade was composed of the 1st and 2nd Armored Regiments, the 24th Lancers and the 10th Dragoons. The 10th Mounted Rifles was the divisional reconnaissance regiment. The first Fireflies were issued to the Division in June 1944. While on 30 June 1944, the Division had a total of 23 Firefly VCs and only 2 ICs, by early April 1945 the ICs outnumbered VCs in all three armored regiments of the Division (23 ICs vs. 16 VCs). [Steven Zaloga Collection]

Sherman IC Firefly

[Right] A disabled Sherman IC Firefly of the 6th South African Armored Division awaiting repairs, guarded by Cape Corps personnel, in the area of Vado, about 20 km south of Bologna, in April 1945. The armored component of the 6th South African Armored Division in Italy in 1944-45 was the 11th South African Armored Brigade that included the Prince Alfred's Guard Regiment, the Pretoria Regiment, the Special Service Battalion, and the Imperial Light Horse/Kimberly Regiment (mot). The Division's armored recce regiment was the Natal Mounted Rifles/SAAF Regiment). [Daniele Guglielmi Collection]

[Continued from page 70]

ner's periscope, which combined a short front rod with a taller double rod rear sight. Some earlier tanks appeared with both metal vane sight and improved sight as a result of upgrades performed at tank depots in the U.S. before the tanks were shipped overseas.

When the gunner's controls were upgraded, the right inside portion of the turret shell casting was thinned down to allow clearance for the sight mechanism. The addition of appliqué armor was approved for this vulnerable area about June 1943.

On the turret roof a removable spotlight was installed that was controllable for traverse and elevation from inside the turret.

Early production turrets were fitted with a pistol port (shell ejection port) in the left side. In February 1943, pistol ports were ordered to be eliminated as soon as possible from the tanks in production. Initially, the holes in the turrets already produced were covered with a welded plug, while intermediate pattern turrets were produced with smooth sides. However, reports from the field requested the pistol port be reinstated, and in July 1943 instructions were received to reintroduce them.

Brush guards fitted to the rotating periscopes appeared for the first time in July 1943.

It was recommended that the British pattern, 2-inch (50.8 mm) bomb thrower, Mk. I (designated M3 2-inch smoke mortar when U.S.-made), be fitted to all production Shermans in June 1943, and it was often retrofitted to earlier turrets before shipment. The mortar was installed in the left front of the

[Right] A South African Hybrid IC of the Prince Alfred's Guard Regiment devoid of any markings. Of interest are the main gun barrel markings, which follow Technical Modification Circular No. A.2135 of 28 June 1944 and the wire lattice for the attachment of camouflage foliage. [Glynn B. Hobbs via William Marshall]

[Left] Shermans of HQ Troop, Pretoria Regiment, taking part in the 6th South African Division's Victory Parade at the Monza Raceway, 14 May 1945. The nearest tank is a Hybrid IC, then Sherman IIA and another Hybrid IC. [Derek Brady via William Marshall]

[Below] A brand new Hybrid IC just taken over by the South African Pretoria Regiment at Prato, Italy, November 1944. No markings have yet been painted on. [Derek Brady via William Marshall]

turret roof at fixed elevation of 35 degrees.

British Shermans

During World War II, Britain received a huge number of U.S.-built medium tanks M4 which formed the backbone of British, Canadian, Polish, New Zealand, South African and Indian armored divisions in all theaters of operations. In all, between May 1942 and October 1944, the United States shipped to the British 2,096 M4 and M4 Composite tanks, 932 M4A1s, 5,041 M4A2s, 7,167 M4A4s, 593 M4(105)s and 1,330 M4A1(76)Ws. For technical evaluation, 7 M4A3s and 5 M4A2(76)Ws were also shipped to Britain, but these tanks were not used operationally.

British designations

The British designated the medium tanks M4, M4A1, M4A2, M4A3 and M4A4 as the Sherman I, II, III, IV and V respectively. The M4 tank fitted the cast upper front hull, known to the U.S. Army as Composite Hull, was designated Sherman I Hybrid by the British. If the armament of the tank was other than the standard 75 mm gun, it was signified by the letter A, B or C (a, b or c in some official wartime British documents), indicating the U.S. 76.2 mm gun, the U.S. 105 mm howitzer or the British 17-pdr respectively. If the tank was fitted with the horizontal volute spring suspension (HVSS), the letter Y was appended to the designation. Thus the M4A4 fitted with the 17-pdr became the Sherman VC, while an M4 fitted with the 17-pdr was designated Sherman IC.

[Left] Tanks of A Troop, Special Services Battalion, 6th South African Armored Division in 1945. The tanks in the center and in the right are Hybrid ICs. The photo shows the main gun camouflage to good effect. Also of note, are the track grousers. [SANDF Archives via William Marshall]

Sherman IC Firefly

[Right] A Sherman IC Hybrid Firefly shortly after issue to 20th Armored Regiment, 4th New Zealand Armored Brigade during a practice shoot at Fabriano, Italy. The 4th New Zealand Infantry Brigade was converted to armor in Egypt in July 1942, with the three infantry battalions (18th, 19th and 20th) becoming armored regiments. Initial plans called for each regiment to be issued with one squadron of Crusaders, one of Grants and one of Shermans but this was changed in mid 1943 and all were issued only with Sherman tanks. The 18th, 19th and 20th Armored Regiments of the Brigade were exclusively equipped with the Sherman IIIs until the arrival of first Fireflies in October 1944. The 4th Armored Brigade embarked at Port Alexandria for Italy, disembarking at Taranto on the 22 October 1943 then moving to the Sangro front, where it first saw action. It fought later at Cassino and took part in the rapid advance to Florence in the summer of 1944, switching to the Adriatic front in 1945, where it ultimately took part in the capture of Trieste in May 1945. [Nigel Overton via Jeffrey Plowman]

[Right] A New Zealand Sherman IC Hybrid Firefly of 18th Armored Regiment crossing a Bailey bridge during the drive north of the Lamone river sometime around 12 December 1944. The combination divisional insignia and unit serial patch appears to have been applied in the center of the rear plate of these tanks. [Tank Museum 2879/A3]

[Left] A Sherman IC Hybrid Firefly (T-268914) of the NZAC Training Depot in Egypt in 1945, being used to provide instruction for reinforcements to the 2nd New Zealand Division. This one is still in its Olive Drab paint and has counter-shading under the front half of the barrel, indicating that it probably saw service in Italy before being transferred to Egypt. [D. McManus via Jeffrey Plowman]

[Left] A Hybrid IC of A Squadron, New Zealand 20th Armored Regiment. The tank has been fitted with a false muzzle brake part way down the barrel. [20th Battalion and Armored Regiment Archives]

[Below] One of two 17-pdr equipped Hybrid ICs (T-269863) of the NZAC Training Depot after the cessation of hostilities in 1945. It was being used to provide instruction for tank troops in the event that a New Zealand force was required in the Far East. This one is still in its Olive Drab paint. The vestiges of the counter-shading under the front half of the barrel are still visible, indicating that it probably saw service in Italy before being transferred to Egypt. The 4th Armored Brigade was initially equipped with Sherman IC Hybrids in late 1944 but later standardized on the Sherman VC, so this is possibly one of the original Sherman ICs issued to the Brigade. [D. McManus via Jeffrey Plowman]

British modifications

Unlike the General Grant tanks, which were fitted with modified turret and armament, the Sherman tanks supplied to Britain were almost identical to U.S. vehicles. They differed only in the installation of British equipment, external stowage, radio sets and antennas and the installation of various stowage bins that were fitted to the turret and the hull.

British and Commonwealth Sherman tanks were equipped with the No. 19 radio set, mounted in the turret bustle. This was consisted of two radios, with each requiring its own aerial. The "A" aerial was installed in the standard socket at the left rear of the turret bustle, and the "B" aerial was fitted in a small socket just to the right of center in the turret bustle roof. The A set aerial could be made from as many as three 4-foot sections of 0.5 in. diameter aerial rod. The B set was always a single 2-foot section.

British tanks which did not have the 2-inch bomb thrower were frequently fitted with two 4-inch (101.6 mm) smoke grenade launchers mounted on the right side of the turret.

Six spare track links were mounted on brackets welded to the glacis, and a towing clevis was fitted to the center of the rear lower hull. Moreover, British tanks were fitted with two external methyl bromide fire extinguishers in addition to the standard internal carbon dioxide equipment. A small external first aid box was fitted to the rear hull plate. British regulations also required a rear view mirror for the driver, mounted on the right front edge of the hull, but these were often omitted in service.

Firefly conversions

Originally, the Challenger, Cruiser Tank (A30), was to be the preferred vehicle when it came to mounting the 17-pdr gun in a tank. By the summer of 1943, however, it became apparent that due to numerous technical problems the Challenger would not be available in sufficient quantity in time for the invasion of Europe, scheduled for mid-1944. As an alternative there were sufficient stocks of U.S. M4 series tanks available and efforts began to install the 17-pdr gun in the standard 75 mm gun turret. The Tank Division of the

Sherman IC Firefly

[Right] Sherman IC Firefly of the 1st Tank Battalion, Czechoslovak Independent Armored Brigade; at Dunkirk in late 1944. The 1st Czechoslovak Armored Brigade was created on 1 September 1943, when the 1st Czechoslovak Independent Brigade converted to armor and was redesignated as the 1st Czechoslovak Independent Armored Brigade Group. The formation continued to train in the U.K. until the summer of 1944 when it moved to Normandy, joining 21st Army Group at Falaise on 30 August. At the beginning of October the brigade advanced to Dunkirk where it relieved Canadian troops besieging the German-held fortress. 1st Brigade spent the remainder of the war at Dunkirk, alternately attacking and being attacked by the German garrison. The Dunkirk garrison did not surrender until 9 May 1945, at which time 15,500 German troops and three U-boats were captured by the Czechoslovaks. The brigade then marched to Prague, reaching the city on 18 May 1945. [Tomas Jambor Collection via Petr Brojo]

Ministry of Supply approved such a conversion following the successful demonstration of an experimental installation, which was constructed in Woolwich Arsenal (London) beginning 26 December 1943. This success was due to the Sherman's large diameter turret ring and the short breech block of the new gun.

Sherman Fireflies used two types of 17-pdr gun, the Mk. IV and Mk. VII, which differed only in the recouperator spring case. In the Firefly, a new elevating system was fitted, giving a range of +20 to –5 degrees. Both manual and power traverse systems were provided. A linkage attached to the turret roof could be locked on the breech ring when the gun was depressed and a barrel travel lock was fitted on the left rear corner of the hull deck.

Due to the increased recoil travel of the 17- pdr, the No. 19 radio set had to be moved from the turret bustle into an armored box welded to the back of the turret bustle. A rectangular hole cut through the rear wall of the turret bustle provided access to the radio set. The armored box was assembled from armor plates 64 mm thick in the rear, 51 mm on the sides, and 25 mm top and bottom. The armored box provided additional space inside the turret and also acted as a counterweight to the increased forward weight of the gun installation. The armored box, together with the long barrel, serves for easy identification of all Firefly variants.

[Left] Sherman IC (T-269736) of the Czechoslovak 1st Tank Battalion; Dunkirk 1944. The Battalion's serial number (51) and the Brigade's badge appear on the final drive cover. [Tomas Jambor Collection via Petr Brojo]

Monthly conversion figures for Fireflies (IC & VC) in 1944	
January	20
February	36
March	54
April	93
May	139
June	176
July	181
August	205
September	268
October	264
November	183
December	164

To make space for additional ammunition stowage the Firefly crew was reduced to four by eliminating the assistant driver/bow gunner, his seat and the bow machine gun. The bow machine gun hole was covered with a welded armored plug. The Firefly carried 77 rounds of 17-pdr ammunition: five ready rounds on the turret basket floor, 14 rounds in the old assistant driver's space, and 58 rounds in three bins under the turret floor. Because of the obstruction caused by the large size of the new breech and recoil guard, an additional hatch for the loader was fitted into the turret roof.

A coaxial 0.30 cal. (7.62 mm) Browning machine gun was mounted to the left of the gun, and a direct sight telescope was mounted to the right. The gunner's periscope was retained.

Firefly production

The War Department's initial production order, placed in January 1944, called for 2,100 Fireflies. The tanks were converted to "C" standards in all available Royal Ordnance Factories including these in Woolwich and Hayes in the London area, Radcliffe near Manchester, and Nottingham, with the first 20 vehicles built in January 1944, and 518 units built by June 1944. The goal was to equip each platoon of each armored regiment with at least two Fireflies as soon as possible. The production tempo reached its peak in September 1944. By January 1945, the British War Department's

[Left] Sherman IC (T-270354) of the Czechoslovak Independent Armored Brigade, Dunkirk; February 1945. [Tomas Jambor Collection via Petr Brojo]

[Right] Sherman IC (T-269310) of the Czechoslovak Independent Armored Brigade, Dunkirk; February 1945. Note the W.D. number crudely painted on the glacis. Initially, the Brigade had only 4 Fireflies (all ICs) on strength, two in each HQ of 1st and 2nd Tank Battalions. In February 1945, the number of ICs increased to 22 reaching a maximum of 34 in late March 1945. All Sherman ICs of the Brigade were exchanged for A30 Challengers prior to the return of the Brigade to Czechoslovakia in May 1945. [Tomas Jambor Collection via Petr Brojo]

Sherman IC Firefly

[Right] Two Sherman ICs of the HQ Company, 1st Tank Battalion, Czechoslovak Independent Armored Brigade; La Panne, Belgium, 17 March 1945. [Tomas Jambor Collection via Petr Brojo]

[Bottom] Sherman IC (T-263592) of the 3 Troop, 3rd Company, 2nd Tank Battalion, Czechoslovak Independent Armored Brigade; Dunkirk, February 1945. The Czechoslovakian forces' national vehicle marking, "CS" in black on a white oval, appears on the rear upper hull plate. [Tomas Jambor Collection via Petr Brojo]

cumulative production orders totaled 3,100 Fireflies, with 1,920 vehicles already delivered. On 31 May 1945, the production orders called for 3,260 vehicles (with 2,139 delivered). The conversion program was cancelled with the end of World War II.

Early in production, most Fireflies were converted from Sherman Vs. When stocks of available Mk Vs were exhausted, further conversions were based on the Sherman I, including a large number of Sherman I Hybrid hulls. The last batches of production vehicles were fitted the British pattern Mk. II All Round Vision cupola for the commander in place of the usual split hatch.

Unit allocation

Supplying converted vehicles to the British, Canadian and Polish armored units which were to be used in Normandy was the first priority. By D-Day, most armored regiments of these units were equipped with 12 Fireflies, enough for one per troop. In most regiments, the Fireflies were parceled out one per troop and the number of vehicles was increased from the traditional three to four per troop. Some regiments kept the Fireflies as a single unit under headquarters control and in combat sent them in batches to stem German counterattacks where needed. The first Fireflies went into action in Normandy in June 1944. On 24 June 1944, the combat units of the 21st Army Group in North-West Europe had 288 Fireflies, with the number increasing to 728 by the end of 1944, and to 1,036 by 30 June 1945.

The allocation of Fireflies to Commonwealth (i.e. British, Canadian, New Zealand, South African) and Polish armored units in Italy were considerably smaller. The first vehicles were available from October 1944, and some were used in combat soon after. In Italy, each platoon was equipped initially with one Firefly at the best, and the total number of operational Fireflies reached only 77 in this area by late 1944, with the number increasing to a total of 225 by 25 June 1945. ☐